Qualifying for Kona:
The Road to the Ironman Triathlon
World Championship in Hawaii

Front Cover: A spirited triathlete enters the run course at the 2009 Ironman Wisconsin, where, each year, 72 athletes qualify to race at the Ironman Triathlon World Championship in Kona.

Other Books by Raymond Britt

Racing Ironman: From Debut to Kona and Beyond

Boston Marathon: The Legendary Course Guide

Epic Ride: Ironman Bike Course Secrets

Racing Ironman Wisconsin

Chicago Marathon

Qualifying for Kona:
The Road to the Ironman Triathlon
World Championship in Hawaii

By Raymond Britt

Published by RunTriMedia Publishing
Chicago IL, Scottsdale AZ, Boston MA

Printed in the United States of America

Visit us at www.RunTriMedia.com and www.RaymondBritt.com

For Wendy, Amanda, Rebecca, Eric and Kirsten

Contents

Introduction

The Destination

- Ironman Kona: What to Expect
- Kona Slots: Races, Allocation, Qualifying Times

Qualifying for Kona

- Training Plan Strategy Year 1
- Kona Slot #1: Ironman USA Lake Placid 2002
- Kona Slot #2: Ironman Wisconsin 2002
- Kona 2002: Debut

Returning to Kona

- Training Plan Strategy Year 2
- Kona Slot #3: Ironman Wisconsin 2003
- Kona 2003: Racing the Sunset

Breaking Barriers

- Training Plan Strategy Year 3
- Kona Slot #4: Ironman USA Lake Placid 2004
- Kona 2004: In Memory of . . .

Principles and Lessons from the Road to Kona

- Structure: Planning Your Season
- Efficiency: How Much Training Time
- Balance: Tracking Your Training
- Execution: Everything Else You Need to Know

Appendix 1: Qualifying Year 1 Training Plan Detail

Appendix 2: Kona Qualifying Races, Times, Divisions

Acknowledgements

The world of endurance events is filled with generous people, communities, and institutions joining together in the spirit of swimming, biking, running, coaching, advising, writing, and more.

My participation in endurance racing, triathlon, and this book, have been inspired and driven by wide spectrum of people both on the course and off of it who joined me for the journey to the finish line and beyond.

My invaluable team of training, racing and supporting partners have included Steve Abbey, Art Hutchinson, Joe Foster, Michael McCormack, Barry Schliesmann, Michael Schiff, John Wragg, Kris Schriesheim, Rob Docherty, Kathy Winkler, Lisa Smith-Batchen, Michael Fisch, Marc Roy at SportStats Timing, Vinu Malik at xtri.com, Jesse Williams and Steve DeKoker at Brooks Sports, Adam Greene at Scott Bikes, Tim Moxey at Nuun, Rob Sleamaker at VasaTrainer, Jeff Banowetz at Competitor Magazine, and many more. I thank you one and all for the exceptional experiences we've shared so far.

My father traveled around the world with me to share many of the racing adventures included in this book, from Canada to Switzerland to Germany and ultimately to Hawaii. His love and support were everlasting, and I still feel his presence on the race course.

Wendy, Amanda, Rebecca, Eric and Kirsten have encouraged, inspired, shared and celebrated the journey with me from the beginning. This book is dedicated to them with unending love and thanks.

Introduction

The first time I saw the Ironman Hawaii World Championship broadcast on television, I knew I wanted to be there myself one day.

I wanted to join the athletes who had competed, struggled, and finally crossed the line in Kona after completing the 2.4 mile, 112 mile bike ride and 26.2 mile marathon. It looked like an epic undertaking, an epic achievement. It looked glorious, it looked painful, and it looked life-changing. I wanted that.

And I wanted the pride that comes with saying I had qualified for, and finished, the Ironman Triathlon World Championship in Kona.

One problem, however. At the time, I had never competed in a triathlon. With no background whatsoever in swimming, biking and running, my getting to Kona seemed just about as likely as my chances to pilot the next space shuttle into outer space.

Soon after that broadcast, I entered a triathlon, and nearly drowned in the 1500 meter swim, which I finished in a dead last 46 minutes. My triathlon dreams just about ended at that point. But somehow, I kept at it.

Two years later, I stood at the starting line of Ironman Canada in Pencticton, British Columbia. My goal was simply to finish. Any thoughts of approaching Kona-caliber speed were nowhere to be found. And with good reason.

I finished in under 12 hours in Canada that year. In the next four years, I competed in other Ironman events, and my finish times were roughly in that same range. Triathletes in my age group were earning Kona slots with times more than an hour faster than me. It seemed like an impossible gap to close.

Not only that, but realistically, even if I did want to close that gap, it would probably involve having to train significantly more time. With a full-time job and a growing family, I just couldn't devote anywhere near the 18-24 hours per week that many books and coaches suggest are required to achieve the Kona dream.

By 2001, I was improving somewhat, and soon I was about 40 minutes away from a qualifying time in my age group. That was close enough to get my attention. I decided I might have a chance to get that much faster, and dedicated myself to increasing speed and performance in the year 2002. But I still had the general training time constraints, so I would have to train better, smarter.

And I did. I trained better, smarter, and faster, and I qualified. Again and again.

By July of 2002 in Lake Placid, I had earned my spot at the 2002 Ironman Triathlon World Championship in Kona. Seven weeks later, I earned a slot in Kona 2003 at Ironman Wisconsin, the first 2003 qualifying race.

In 2003, I returned to Ironman Wisconsin and finished 6th in my age group, securing my spot in Kona for 2004.

In 2004, I knocked 21 minutes off of my Ironman PR in Lake Placid, finishing well into the group of Kona qualifiers, but having already qualified, I did not need that slot. I was happy enough to take pride in a new personal best.

This book is all about my training and racing years from 2002 to 2004, including the training plans, the race reports, the Kona qualifiers and the Kona experience. It includes every detail of every day I trained combined with an overall review of the years' training and racing strategies. It shares my path to Kona, a long way from that first triathlon with the 46 minute 1500 meter swim.

As a friend likes to say: your mileage may vary. Not everything I do in training and racing is right for everyone.

For example, I race more than most, and train less than most, for example. My rationale for that: racing is great training, and I plan my race schedule to increase speed and endurance on a path to my Ironman races.

Another example, I tend not to do many 'easy' workouts. Time is precious, I try to make the most of it. Also, I tend not to taper very much, unless it's a very important race, like a Kona qualifying attempt.

As mentioned above, I do not subscribe to the notion that a tremendous about of training time is necessary to reach qualifying potential.

And I'll also assure you that I don't have some hidden advantage, as if I was a high school state champ swimmer or something like that. Believe me, I could barely swim. As a teenager, I only rode my bike to school, and I could not run because I needed corrective shoes and had asthma.

Everything I've accomplished in endurance athletics began when I was 34 years old. And now that includes three trips to Kona, and three glorious finishes.

Enjoy the Journey.

Notes about the content: I wrote the annual training and racing reviews and race reports shortly after the events themselves, and I have decided to not change them in places that may make them look dated today (for example, referring to 'last year' means the year before the time I was writing, etc.).

Destination

- Ironman Kona: What to Expect
- Kona Slots: Races, Allocation, Qualifying Times

Ironman Kona: What to Expect

Each October, many of the world's best long-distance triathletes from all over the planet will find themselves on the exciting descent into Kona International airport. During that landing, the athletes will get a glimpse of the course they will race on, during the 2007 Ironman Triathlon World Championship.

Many athletes will be returning to the Big Island, they know what to expect already. But for hundreds of athletes who earned their starting slot at qualifying races in the previous year, race day will be a new experience.

If you're one of the rookies, what can you expect in Kona on race day?

I competed in Kona in 2002, 2003, and 2004. I had dreamt of earning my spot to Kona for years, then diligently trained to get there. After finally earning my slot at Ironman USA Lake Placid, the excitement I felt about just going to Kona was enough.

The excitement builds as race day approaches. The Carbo Load dinner joins the community of athletes under the stars and you feel as if there is no other place you should be at that moment.

It's almost enough, just being there. The reward is picking up your bib number. The race might almost seem an afterthought. But there's still an Ironman triathlon, on of the toughest ones in the world, to complete.

Race Day – Pre-Dawn

The Kona Ironman morning routine will be much like your other pre-race experiences, but this one will have a couple of differences. First. you will have to line-up to get formally body-marked – it's a real process — and the line does not move quickly. It you are the kind that needs plenty of extra time in the transition area to feel relaxed, get to body-marking very early.

Second, there will be television camera crews surrounding the athletes, focusing specifically on the pros and a few pre-selected age groupers. It's the beginning of everything you've seen on the television broadcasts of the race. There's Natascha Badmann . . . there's Craig Alexander . . . It will strike you at that moment: This is Real, I am Here. The fun begins.

There's only one thing to worry about: getting in the water before the cannon fires at 7am. The very narrow stair entrance to the ocean at Dig Me Beach means that it's a single-file process. The line can extend even farther than the bodymarking line did. If you need to be in the water comfortably a few minutes before the race starts, get there early.

Swim

There is no Ironman swim that is as enjoyable as the one in Kailua-Kona Bay. Unless rough water conditions have churned up the sandy bottom, as happened in 2002, the water is clear and the views are spectacular.

When you're in the water before the start, just look around. It's an amazing moment. You are really there. It's everything you expected it would be. Then . . . boom! And cheers. Off you go.

As you work your way into a good rhythm in the water, you'll start to notice that you're among a good, even polite, group of swimmers. Maybe this is more true for the slower swimmers, like me. In other Ironman races, with up to 2500 people in the water at the same time, the congestion can be unreal, the constant contact frustrating.

But in Kona, you only seem to be around good swimmers, ones who know where they are going, who don't bang into you. You'll find the swim experience enjoyable because you're really swimming with a group of swimmers like you. It's like a group run, you'll enjoy the company of others around you. It will be a new experience.

And make sure you look down often to take in the scenery. It can be wonderful, and even distracting. But worth it. That's the part of the swim you'll remember most.

Others who know better tell me that the Kona swim is typically breezy out to the turnaround, followed by a tougher return. The return to shore has been likened to a 'water treadmill'; you don't move forward as fast as you think. No matter, you're there for the experience. Enjoy it.

Bike

One of the things I looked most forward to was the 112 mile ride through the lava fields. It looked like a spiritual experience as I watched it on television broadcasts, and it was exactly like that when I got there in person. But first, you have to get there.

I break the Kona bike course into five parts: warmup, fast and fun, legendary climb, screaming downhill, headwinds going home.

Warm up

The first several miles of the bike course, in and around the town of Kona, seem to be designed to break up the pack somewhat. There are small climbs and descents that basically give cyclists the opportunity to warm up without going crazy. The first miles are such that you won't see a lot of passing, and you'll realize it's best to just hold your position and get into a comfortable cycling rhythm.

Fast and Fun: to Waikoloa

When you get onto the Queen K highway, the best part of the bike course is ahead of you. The highway is nicely paved, the undulations are friendly and not too challenging. You're fresh and you'll feel like picking up the pace a little. Go ahead. Just keep it in check; tougher miles are ahead.

Look right, left and forward. All you will see is dried lava. You're out in the middle of nowhere, and it'll be nearly silent, except for the sound of cyclists pedaling. Mile-after-mile through fields that feel like an endless moonscape. Where else will you ever have an experience like that? It's where you were meant to be.

Your bike computer will say are fast, having a great ride. And that will be a true impression for the first hour or two. But when you reach the intersection for Waikoloa Village, it's time for some serious work.

Legendary Climb 'The Road to Hawi . . .'

After Waikoloa, the course will toss some sharp drops and climbs in the next few miles. And then you will take a left turn toward the west side of the island, for the climb to Hawi.

Check it out on the course map, there's a point where the climb clearly begins, 12 miles before the top. Mile markers on the road will measure your progress. But they will creep toward you, not as fast as you might want them to. You start the climb thinking: 12 miles, that's not too bad. And yes, it could be worse, but it's not easy. Take this time to eat and hydrate if you can.

The last five miles to Hawi are more exposed to wind, and you may have to battle that additional resistance. Gravity and wind. Not fun. But soon you'll be in Hawi, an unremarkable town but for the role it plays in the Ironman. Then you're heading downhill.

Screaming Downhill: into the Wind

What goes up, must come down. And after Hawi, you will retrace the course back downhill. It's a manageable downhill, not so fast that you have to concentrate closely on staying in control. But it's fast enough to help you gain back some of that speed you lost on the earlier climb.

The bad news is that it's only 12 miles or so downhill. Then things get a little challenging on the next 13 miles heading back toward Waikoloa. The wind may be getting stronger, and it's all but certain to be blowing right at you.

Headwinds Going Home

You'll reach the Waikoloa intersection feeling pretty good, and your bike computer might reveal that you're having a good ride, speed and time. Each time I got there, I was thinking: hold this pace, and you'll finish near a bike PR!

No such luck in any of those cases. While the last 25 miles are relatively flat, it's the pummeling headwinds that will all but kill those dreams. I remember riding 12 to 15 miles per hour, and just not being able to pick up the pace.

The winds are maddening. And the mile markers are there, again, constantly reminding you how far you have not gone. Just hang in there. Everyone is dealing with the same conditions. Everyone will tell the same story when the race is over: the winds were everything you heard they would be. Rough.

Run

In 2004, I remember emerging from bike-to-run transition into a blast furnace of the most powerful heat I'd ever experienced on a race course. By the time you start running, the sun will be high in the sky, the humidity will feel like 100%, and the asphalt will be radiating even more heat.

It takes time to acclimate to that kind of heat after swimming 2.4 miles and riding 112. The good news is that first half of the course provides many opportunities to run in the shade, while soaking yourself with ice and sponges at well-stocked aid stations.

After heading east out of town on Alii Drive, the course takes you to an oceanfront turnaround near the 6 mile point. You'll do a 180 degree turn and head back toward town. The run course is mostly flat for the first 12 miles or so. Then you're back in town, facing Palani Drive.

A friend and consistent top age-group finisher in Kona tells me: the race begins at Palani Drive. For him, he's been running the first half of the marathon smartly. He turns it up a notch or two after he runs the 200 yards up Palani, then heads west on the Queen K.

If you want to be competitive in Kona, he is indeed right. The last 13.1 miles in Kona are where the best crack wide open. You are completely exposed to the sun. There are long inclines to wear you down. And yes, for some reason, the several miles into and out of the Energy Lab can suck the life out of you. The competitive racers will use those challenges to their advantage.

The rest of us – I race Kona for fun – can expect to run more conservatively, trying to maintain pace. The Energy Lab may not seem as rough as it does in Ironman broadcasts; it is survivable. Once you're past that, 21 miles complete, just 5 miles to town, and you're an Ironman.

The next four miles have never been easy for me. They seem to be constantly uphill, and they go by so slowly. But when you reach Palani Drive, and make that right hand turn after the 25 mile marker, your best moments are ahead.

Finish

Savor that last mile. You will have trained and raced thousands of miles over the years to get there, For the first 1000 meters of it, you will probably be alone. Most of the spectators are at the finish line. In that relative solitude, reflect on all you've done to get to that point.

Two right turns later, and you're on Alii Drive. Sacred Ground. At first you won't see the finish line, but you'll hear it. You keep going. Then you see the bright lights, you hear Mike Reilly welcoming home the athletes ahead of you.

Then it's your turn. The best 100 yards in endurance sports. Slow down. High five spectators, cross the line with your favorite gesture as Mike Reilly says it:

You are An Ironman!

Kona Slots: Races, Allocation, Times

Each year, more than 50,000 triathletes compete in races all over the world hoping to earn one of roughly 1800 golden opportunities of a lifetime: the right to race with the best in the world in Kona.

The allocation of those 1800 slots is roughly as follows

- 1500 slots earned at qualifying races (see next page)
- 200 awarded in an official Ironman lottery held each Spring; thousands apply; see www.ironman.com for details and registration
- The rest go to previous Kona winners, last year's Kona age group winners, NBC broadcast subjects, sponsor and manufacturer representatives.

Other than trying your luck – against very long odds --at the lottery, if you want to go to Kona, you need to qualify. An overview of the qualifying slot distribution process:

- The 1500 slots are allocated among 25 Ironman qualifying races and Ironman 70.3 California
- The slots each race gets (e.g., Wisconsin = 72 slots) are allocated among age-group divisions and pros (e.g., M45-49 age group gets 6 slots)
- The slots in each race's age-group division are reserved for the top finishers (e.g., the top 6 finishers in M45-49 are entitled to take a slot)
- It may happen that some athletes will choose to not accept a slot they earned for some reason; any slots not accepted 'roll down' to the next finisher(s) who also have the option to accept or pass on the slot.
- The 'Roll Down' process continues until all slots are taken
- Note: see official race rules for details and timing

The following pages provide more detailed examples.

Ironman Races with Kona Slots in 2010

Race	Kona Slots	Race Date
Ironman Malaysia	36	2/27/2010
Ironman New Zealand	75	3/6/2010
Ironman China	50	3/14/2010
Ironman Australia	60	3/28/2010
Ironman South Africa	30	4/25/2010
Ironman St. George	65	5/1/2010
Ironman Lanzarote	60	5/22/2010
Ironman Brazil	50	5/30/2010
Ironman Japan	50	6/13/2010
Ironman France	35	6/27/2010
Ironman Coeur d'Alene	65	6/27/2010
Ironman Germany	120	7/4/2010
Ironman Austria	50	7/4/2010
Ironman Switzerland	72	7/25/2010
Ironman Lake Placid	72	7/25/2010
Ironman Regensburg	50	8/1/2010
Ironman UK	30	8/1/2010
Ironman Louisville	72	8/29/2010
Ironman Canada	72	8/29/2010
Ironman Wisconsin*	72	9/12/2010
Ironman World Championship		10/9/2010
Ironman Florida*	72	11/6/2010
Ironman Arizona*	72	11/21/2010
Ironman Cozumel*	50	11/28/2010
Ironman Western Australia*	40	12/4/2010

* Slots for Kona 2011

Kona Slot Allocation Within Each Race

As you're deciding which race to choose, you'll also need to consider then next degree of difficulty: the limited number of Kona qualifying slots per age group in each race.

Your age on race day will put you in one of several 5-year span age divisions, e.g., at age 48, you would compete in the 45-49 Division.

The total number of available slots per race are allocated among the Age Divisions and Pro athletes using the following guidelines as described at ironmanusa.com:

"At least one Kona slot shall be allocated IN FULL-DISTANCE EVENTS to each five-year age-group category in which any age group athlete sends in an application, both male and female, per the age group categories listed.

Be aware that some age groups may be combined for the allocation of a Kona slot at the sole discretion of the race director. If there are no athletes entered in the race in a particular age group, then that slot will be moved to the largest populated age group in that same gender. For additional age group slots, slot allocation shall be representative of the actual number of age group applicants in each category in the race.

As an example, if 8% of the age-group applicants are females 40-44, then 8% of these slots would be allocated in the female 40-44 category. Please note that at 10 percent of Ford Ironman World Championship slots at full-distance events are allocated to Professionals i.e. 80 qualifying spots, eight are reserved for pros.

Note: All athletes must be present at Hawaii Registration to claim their spot."

**Recent North American Ironman Races:
Kona Slots Allocated by Division**

Division	IM AZ	IM CA	IM CD	IM FL	IM LP	IM WI
M18-24	1	1	1	2	1	3
M25-29	3	3	4	3	3	4
M30-34	7	5	6	6	5	7
M35-39	10	8	8	8	8	9
M40-44	11	8	9	9	9	8
M45-49	7	7	7	7	8	6
M50-54	5	5	4	5	5	4
M55-59	2	3	2	2	3	2
M60-64	1	2	1	1	1	1
M65-69	1	1	1	1	1	1
M70-74	1		1	1	1	1
M75-79	1			1		
MPRO	6	5	4	5	4	4
W18-24	1	1	1	1	1	1
W25-29	2	2	3	2	2	3
W30-34	4	3	3	3	4	3
W35-39	4	4	4	4	3	4
W40-44	4	4	4	3	4	3
W45-49	3	3	3	3	3	2
W50-54	2	2	1	1	2	1
W55-59	1	1	1	1	1	1
W60-64	1	1	1	1		1
W75+		1				
WPRO	2	2	3	2	3	3
Grand Total	80	72	72	72	72	72

Kona Qualifying Times

Very few slots per Division, it turns out. And the difficulty doesn't stop there.

Up to 2500 triathletes compete in each race. Things get tougher: in the highly popular Divisions, between ages 30-34, 35-39, 40-44, 45-49, and 50-54, for example, you'll need to finish among the top 3% or so of the group.

For the real Reality Check: look at the times turned in by the athletes that qualified for Kona in each of these five North American Ironman races (a sample is on the opposite page; complete lists are in the Appendix).

Note: do not get discouraged when you see some extraordinary times posted by athletes in your age Division.

Don't let yourself be intimidated if you feel the gap between your current performance and ability and target qualifying times is too great.

You want to improve, you want to know the goals you're shooting for. If the goal is Kona – and it is if you're reading this – this is the starting point.

Most importantly, remember: every qualifying athlete listed on the following pages at one point could only dream of winning a Kona slot. Through hard and efficient training, they achieved the goal. With determination and perseverance, you will, too

Ironman Arizona 2008 Qualifying Times

Division	Swim	T1	Bike	T2	Run	Total
M18-24	1:03:56	4:16	4:55:16	2:38	3:24:17	9:30:22
M25-29	52:37:00	4:24	4:44:44	1:55	3:08:57	8:52:36
M25-29	55:31:00	4:19	4:59:55	1:33	3:11:29	9:12:45
M25-29	57:41:00	4:41	4:48:50	2:22	3:24:22	9:17:54
M30-34	50:08:00	3:29	4:57:29	2:52	3:14:25	9:08:21
M30-34	56:41:00	3:31	4:56:46	0:59	3:14:04	9:11:58
M30-34	1:01:00	4:01	4:55:02	1:12	3:11:31	9:12:45
M30-34	1:00:57	3:08	5:09:59	1:11	3:13:11	9:28:24
M30-34	56:35:00	4:30	4:59:33	1:54	3:27:16	9:29:46
M30-34	59:38:00	4:11	4:55:47	1:56	3:28:28	9:29:59
M30-34	59:01:00	5:47	5:11:41	3:08	3:14:38	9:34:13
M35-39	1:00:03	4:01	4:57:35	2:36	3:11:16	9:15:28
M35-39	50:23:00	4:45	5:01:30	2:44	3:22:06	9:21:26
M35-39	1:01:12	4:01	5:03:12	2:14	3:11:25	9:22:01
M35-39	1:03:48	4:27	4:58:25	2:25	3:14:01	9:23:05
M35-39	56:55:00	4:15	5:10:36	1:30	3:16:10	9:29:25
M35-39	1:07:07	5:16	5:02:36	3:34	3:12:44	9:31:15
M35-39	1:03:46	4:59	4:55:19	1:41	3:26:04	9:31:47
M35-39	58:35:00	4:42	5:07:16	2:56	3:26:36	9:40:03
M35-39	1:02:34	4:34	5:10:05	1:47	3:21:42	9:40:41
M35-39	1:02:12	4:19	5:05:43	1:37	3:30:38	9:44:27
M40-44	50:24:00	3:30	4:56:06	1:47	3:19:53	9:11:38
M40-44	59:58:00	3:37	4:57:40	2:07	3:20:22	9:23:41
M40-44	1:02:17	4:42	5:02:30	3:23	3:11:51	9:24:39
M40-44	53:42:00	4:49	4:51:25	3:10	3:36:06	9:29:11
M40-44	1:01:57	3:41	4:58:18	2:33	3:32:02	9:38:30
M40-44	51:45:00	4:17	5:10:56	3:37	3:32:48	9:43:21
M40-44	57:02:00	4:49	5:07:39	2:20	3:34:48	9:46:36
M40-44	1:05:17	4:04	5:05:27	1:38	3:32:34	9:48:58
M40-44	1:10:08	4:28	5:03:36	3:20	3:30:37	9:52:07
M40-44	1:04:23	4:23	5:06:30	1:34	3:37:12	9:54:01
M40-44	1:05:05	5:05	4:59:18	2:07	3:42:39	9:54:13
M45-49	56:18:00	5:35	4:59:43	2:58	3:30:52	9:35:24
M45-49	59:35:00	5:34	5:15:41	1:43	3:22:54	9:45:25
M45-49	1:09:32	5:57	5:05:19	1:42	3:25:33	9:48:01
M45-49	1:01:33	3:44	4:56:16	1:46	3:45:52	9:49:09
M45-49	1:11:45	4:47	5:05:22	2:23	3:28:05	9:52:20
M45-49	59:14:00	3:30	5:18:07	2:09	3:30:21	9:53:19
M45-49	1:07:20	6:40	5:06:00	2:36	3:30:57	9:53:32

All these factors considered, it's not at all easy to qualify for Kona these days. And it gets harder each year as times get faster.

There is hope. Even if you're not blessed with inborn talent as a swimmer, cyclist, or runner. You can get there, It just takes time, determination, and focus.

The next three sections take you though the regular athlete's evolution from rookie to Kona Ironman. It can be your story, too.

Qualifying

- Qualifying Training Plan Strategy Year 1
- Kona Slot #1: Ironman USA Lake Placid 2002
- Kona Slot #2: Ironman Wisconsin 2002
- Kona 2002: Debut

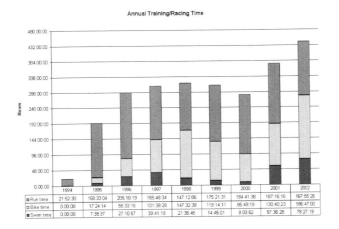

Annual Training/Racing Time

	1994	1995	1996	1997	1998	1999	2000	2001	2002
Run time	21:52:30	168:33:04	205:10:19	165:48:34	147:12:06	175:21:31	184:41:38	187:16:16	167:55:26
Bike time	0:00:00	17:24:14	55:33:16	101:38:28	147:32:39	119:14:11	86:49:19	130:40:23	196:47:00
Swim time	0:00:00	7:38:37	27:10:57	39:41:19	21:36:45	14:45:01	9:03:52	57:36:26	78:27:19

Qualifying Training Plan Strategy Year 1

After several plateau racing performance years, 2002 was a breakthrough year, including a 2:54 Boston Marathon and qualifying for Kona 2002 and 2003. Looking at my 2002 training log, it's easy to see the changes I made in training to achieve this new level of performance.

First, some background, for perspective. As of 2002, I was 42 years old, married 18 years with four kids, and had a busy job as a marketing/strategy executive. I never had – and will never have – the kind of hours available that people tend to put in to be their best at Ironman racing. So I had to make do. My program may not be right for everybody, but it worked for me.

From 1997 to 2000, I pretty much proved that if I trained an average of 6 hours per week – roughly 1 hour swimming, 2.5 hours biking, 2.5 hours running -- I could complete Ironman triathlons in the 11 to 12 hour range. In fact, I completed eleven of them. It was great to get the finisher's medals, but I wasn't progressing.

In 2001, I stepped up the volume, averaging about 7.25 hours training, with a little more emphasis on cycling, and began to close the Kona qualification gap. 2001 ended with 57 hours and 103 miles swimming; 130 hours and 2463 miles cycling; and 187 hours and 1522 miles running.

In November 2001 at Ironman Florida, I broke the 11 hour barrier to finish in 10:40. This was 40 minutes from a Kona slot, but it was closer than I had ever been before.

I decided that to shave enough time to qualify for Kona 2002, I needed to redouble my effort on cycling, and run less, but faster. I also needed to achieve a better balance of training, timing and equipment.

By year-end 2002, I had increased swimming by 41% to 78 hours and 146 miles; biking by 55% to 196 hours and 3830 miles, and had cut back my running by 11% to 167 hours and 1347 miles.

In an average week in 2002, I swam 90 minutes, biked 3.75 hours for 73 miles, and ran 3.15 hours and 26 miles. This translated to adding an average of 1.25 hours per week compared with 2001, for a total of 8.5 hours per week.

Training Summary 1997 to 2002: Core Data

Swim, Bike, Run

	1997	1998	1999	2000	2001	2002
Miles	3,056.5	3,803.3	3,502.2	2,928.4	4,089.2	5,324.8
Time	307:08:21	316:21:30	309:20:43	279:34:49	375:33:07	443:09:45
Sessions	282	289	261	259	366	390
Distance/Session	10.8	13.2	13.4	11.3	11.2	13.65
Time/session	1:05:21	1:05:41	1:11:07	1:04:46	1:01:34	1:08:11
Time/mile	06:02	04:59	05:18	05:44	05:31	04:59.6
Time/week	5:54:23	6:05:02	5:56:56	5:22:36	7:12:09	8:31:20

Swim

	1997	1998	1999	2000	2001	2002
Miles	68.9	38.2	27.4	15.3	103.5	146.3
Time	39:41:19	21:36:45	14:45:01	9:03:52	57:36:28	78:27:19
Sessions	59	36	26	13	96	121
Distance/Session	1.2	1.1	1.1	1.2	1.1	1.21
Time/session	0:40:22	0:36:01	0:34:02	0:41:50	0:36:00	0:38:54
Time/mile	34:32	0:33:57	0:32:17	0:35:32	0:33:24	32:10.2

Bike

	1997	1998	1999	2000	2001	2002
Miles	1,781.5	2,667.9	2,276.1	1,525.8	2,463.6	3,830.8
Time	101:38:28	147:32:39	119:14:11	85:49:19	130:40:23	196:47:00
Sessions	78	120	101	70	107	129
Distance/Session	22.8	22.2	22.5	21.8	23.0	29.70
Time/session	1:18:11	1:13:46	1:10:50	1:13:34	1:13:16	1:31:32
Time/mile	03:25	03:19	03:09	03:22	03:11	03:04.9

Run

	1997	1998	1999	2000	2001	2002
Miles	1,206.0	1,097.2	1,198.7	1,387.3	1,522.1	1,347.7
Time	165:48:34	147:12:06	175:21:31	184:41:38	187:16:16	167:55:26
Sessions	145	133	134	176	163	140
Distance/Session	8.3	8.2	8.9	7.9	9.3	9.63
Time/session	1:08:37	1:06:24	1:18:31	1:02:58	1:08:56	1:11:58
Time/mile	08:15	0:08:03	0:08:47	0:07:59	0:07:23	07:28.6

Periodization

My weekly training varied to appropriately build up to each major race, with a generally decent taper beforehand (though I tend to taper less than most), and a reasonable recovery period afterwards. This is obvious from looking at the chart of my weekly training time.

The builds to each major event -- Ironman New Zealand in week 9, Ironman USA in week 31, Ironman Wisconsin in week 38, then Ironman Hawaii in week 42 -- are pretty clear in the chart.

A few things are notable particularly the 24 week build to my qualifying race in Lake Placid. After recovering from Ironman New Zealand briefly, I entered marathon season in April (Boston) and May (Mad City Marathon), but wrapped additional cycling in most weeks, to build from 7-hour training weeks to 12 hour training weeks by June. You can also see how the running receded, making way for more cycling time in early summer. Also, I undertook a very real two-week taper just before Ironman USA, my first one ever. And it paid dividends.

After Ironman USA, my training weeks were less consistent, as I was listening to my body. When it said rest, I did. But it appears that the buildup for Ironman USA held, as I was able to run a 2003 qualifying race seven weeks later in Wisconsin.

Training Summary 1997-2002: Annual Changes

Swim, Bike, Run

	1998	1999	2000	2001	2002
Miles	24%	-8%	-16%	40%	30%
Time	3%	-2%	-10%	34%	18%
Sessions	2%	-10%	-1%	41%	7%
Distance/Session	21%	2%	-16%	-1%	22%
Time/session	1%	8%	-9%	-5%	11%
Time/mile	-17%	6%	8%	-4%	-9%
Time/week	3%	-2%	-10%	34%	18%

Swim

	1998	1999	2000	2001	2002
Miles	-45%	-28%	-44%	576%	41%
Time	-46%	-32%	-39%	536%	36%
Sessions	-39%	-28%	-50%	638%	26%
Distance/Session	-9%	-1%	12%	-8%	12%
Time/session	-11%	-6%	23%	-14%	8%
Time/mile	-2%	-5%	10%	-6%	-4%
Time/week	-46%	-32%	-39%	536%	36%

Bike

	1998	1999	2000	2001	2002
Miles	50%	-15%	-33%	61%	55%
Time	45%	-19%	-28%	52%	51%
Sessions	54%	-16%	-31%	53%	21%
Distance/Session	-3%	1%	-3%	6%	29%
Time/session	-6%	-4%	4%	0%	25%
Time/mile	-3%	-5%	7%	-6%	-3%
Time/week	45%	-19%	-28%	52%	51%

Run

	1998	1999	2000	2001	2002
Miles	-9%	9%	16%	10%	-11%
Time	-11%	19%	5%	1%	-10%
Sessions	-8%	1%	31%	-7%	-14%
Distance/Session	-1%	8%	-12%	18%	3%
Time/session	-3%	18%	-20%	9%	4%
Time/mile	-2%	9%	-9%	-8%	1%
Time/week	-11%	19%	5%	1%	-10%

Key Differences

In addition to more training time, I did several things differently than in previous years.

First, I cycled more than 1500 indoor miles on my CompuTrainer in the winter months. These sessions varied from 30 minutes to more than 5 hours, from strength and speed work to long endurance rides. In early 2002, I made sure to ride at least 56 miles on CompuTrainer once per week. The physical and mental training was awesome. These winter indoor training miles, utilizing the heart rate, cadence and wattage feedback, brought me into the spring season strong and fast.

Second, I did nearly a complete reversal after running Boston in 2:54 in April. My friend and xtri contributor, Art Hutchinson, had a thought, and he wasn't kidding: 'you've proven you can run, so why don't you substitute serious rides for your planned runs, and cut back your running to basic maintenance.' By years' end, I was still able to comfortably run a 3:05 Chicago Marathon, though I was running much than 25 miles per week in training.

Third, I lived on my Softride as soon as it got warm enough to train regularly outside. As much as I would miss running, Art was right, and it is obvious in my training log. Morning runs were skipped in favor of regular 27 mile rides at dawn. My average ride distance increased from 23 miles in 2002 to 29 in 2003.

The increased time in the saddle began to yield dividends, and surprisingly, I wasn't losing my running speed. In fact, I was gaining - - I finished top 4 in a local half marathon in June, with a PR time of 1:22. This is not surprising if you look at my logs over time: I have become a faster runner running fewer miles and spending more time on the bike.

2002 Weekly Training Mix: Time

Weekly Time

Sum of Time	Type			
Week	Bike	Run	Swim	Grand Total
1	3:12:26	1:55:00	3:00:47	8:08:13
2	9:44:55	2:41:58	0:59:59	13:26:52
3	4:32:42	1:37:47	3:02:44	9:13:13
4	6:15:00	5:33:03	3:56:08	15:44:11
5	3:30:00	0:40:00	1:27:16	5:37:16
6	4:00:00	5:35:22	3:27:57	13:03:19
7	1:30:00	4:20:11	2:02:11	7:52:22
8	4:51:00	1:34:47	3:02:39	9:28:26
9	6:34:36	4:22:44	1:09:42	12:07:02
10	0:30:00	1:40:20	1:33:47	3:44:07
11	1:00:00	3:14:08	1:04:49	5:18:57
12		4:42:58	1:02:02	5:45:00
13		8:01:56	2:31:00	10:32:56
14	2:32:30	6:15:24	1:41:33	10:29:27
15	0:59:00	4:47:15	1:32:04	7:18:19
16	2:53:00	3:54:27	1:36:48	8:24:15
17	6:10:00		1:32:31	7:42:31
18	3:08:22	4:11:28	1:35:07	8:54:57
19	3:02:24	5:15:57	2:16:23	10:34:44
20	5:48:02	3:33:13	3:02:00	12:23:15
21	1:59:05	3:04:20	0:31:54	5:35:19
22	5:00:50	3:27:36	1:09:35	9:38:01
23	7:38:03	1:27:42	3:19:13	12:24:58
24	6:32:58	2:29:50	1:44:35	10:47:23
25	7:57:24	3:24:29	0:20:29	11:42:22
26	3:46:40	5:01:34	2:38:08	11:26:22
27	10:07:17	2:57:04	0:43:44	13:48:05
28	6:46:37	2:49:06	2:32:53	12:08:36
29	3:19:24	3:15:08	0:41:02	7:15:34
30	3:51:50	1:05:46	0:44:47	5:42:23
31	9:42:10	4:34:25	1:31:20	15:47:55
32	4:53:27	1:54:01	2:11:00	8:58:28
33	3:36:42	5:46:02	1:33:25	10:56:09
34	5:09:00	3:10:06	2:30:21	10:49:27
35		1:47:08	0:34:06	2:21:14
36	3:39:45	1:06:42	1:34:12	6:20:39
37	1:40:20	2:28:02	0:39:53	4:48:15
38	7:14:15	3:36:16	2:07:39	12:58:10
39	2:11:18	3:15:45	1:33:30	7:00:33
40	6:26:55	1:39:33	0:15:10	8:21:38
41	3:01:48	2:02:38	1:01:20	6:05:46
42	6:01:54	6:55:46	1:33:41	14:31:21
43		0:45:32		0:45:32
44	0:30:00	0:27:08	0:51:22	1:48:30
45		1:06:01	0:57:40	2:03:41
46	1:32:36	3:31:48		5:04:24
47	2:08:36	1:00:46	0:29:44	3:39:06
48	2:15:00	5:13:42		7:28:42
49	2:04:20	1:56:57	0:58:00	4:59:17
50	1:50:30	3:17:09	2:01:09	7:08:48
51	2:00:30	1:41:28		3:41:58
52	3:33:49	3:28:48		7:02:37
53		4:09:10		4:09:10
Grand Total	196:47:00	167:55:26	78:27:19	443:09:45

Fourth, for the first time ever, I was able to get through the season without running injury. As a serious overpronator, I've always needed stabilization shoes, but couldn't settle on the right one. In 2002 I found it, and ran 1300 miles on five different pairs of Brooks Trance shoes. In my 2002 training log I tracked how many miles per pair, so I would know when to switch pairs. I've learned through this analysis that I need to switch somewhere around 300 miles to stay injury free.

The best part of a detailed review of the past year's (and even before that) training logs, is that they allow you to decipher what worked, what didn't, what you need to keep, and what you need to change as you launch your assault on the 2003 season.

	Time	Miles	Workou
Softride Outdoor Rides	117:28:43	2,295.0	6!
CompuTrainer Indoor Rides	79:38:10	1,536.4	6!
Brooks Trance Outdoor Runs	155:20:24	1,270.1	11!
Treadmill Indoor Runs	9:41:12	55.2	1(
Lap Pool Swims	68:35:04	127.7	10
Outdoor Swims	5:21:34	10.5	!
Other	7:04:38	30.0	1:
Total	443:09:45	5,324.8	39(

2002 Weekly Training Mix: Distance

Weekly Distance

Sum of Dist	Type				
Week	Bike	Run	Swim	(blank)	Grand Total
1	58.6	14.2	5.4		78.3
2	193.8	23.1	1.8		218.8
3	91.9	12.8	5.5		110.2
4	123.1	46.0	7.4		176.4
5	64.3	4.7	2.7		71.7
6	79.4	42.9	6.4		128.6
7	29.7	35.3	3.7		68.7
8	90.5	12.0	5.5		108.0
9	129.0	32.5	2.4		163.9
10	10.0	13.4	2.8		26.2
11	18.1	27.1	1.9		47.1
12		39.4	1.9		41.3
13		54.0	4.5		58.5
14	48.5	51.4	3.2		103.1
15	20.0	41.7	2.9		64.6
16	51.2	35.3	2.9		89.3
17	115.3		2.8		118.2
18	56.8	32.9	3.0		92.7
19	54.4	44.4	4.3		103.1
20	111.7	26.2	5.6		143.4
21	40.0	27.3	1.0		68.3
22	99.3	29.3	2.2		130.8
23	148.4	11.5	6.5		166.4
24	132.1	22.5	3.3		157.9
25	161.4	28.4	0.7		190.4
26	70.8	40.2	5.1		116.0
27	202.4	25.8	1.4		229.6
28	131.8	24.4	4.8		161.0
29	67.7	26.5	1.3		95.5
30	78.2	9.1	1.3		88.6
31	193.9	34.8	3.1		231.8
32	86.7	16.7	4.0		107.4
33	75.2	49.2	3.0		127.4
34	101.7	26.0	4.8		132.5
35		13.9	1.1		15.0
36	69.0	8.6	2.9		80.5
37	32.9	21.6	1.3		55.8
38	142.6	26.2	4.0		172.8
39	44.3	26.3	2.9		73.5
40	114.5	13.0	0.5		128.0
41	60.3	18.8	1.9		81.0
42	112.0	52.4	2.9		167.3
43		6.0			6.0
44	9.0	3.6	1.6		14.2
45		8.5	1.8		10.3
46	30.0	24.6			54.6
47	45.0	9.1	0.9		55.0
48	46.8	40.3			87.1
49	41.0	13.6	1.8		56.4
50	31.8	24.0	3.7		59.5
51	41.4	13.9			55.3
52	74.4	27.3			101.7
53		35.3			35.3
Grand Total	3830.8	1347.7	146.3		5324.8

2002 Training Summary: Key Differences

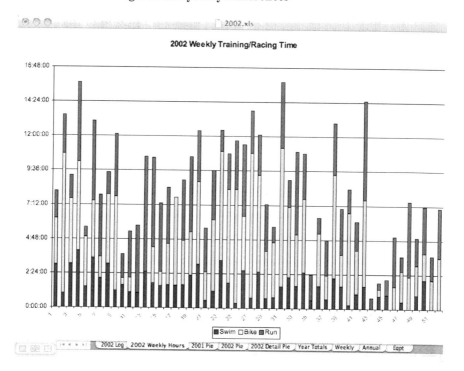

Kona Slot #1: Ironman USA Lake Placid 2002

My Ironman experience, from the first one in 1997, until late last year, can be summarized by words from Lance Armstrong's book, It's Not About the Bike:

"People ask me why I ride my bike for six hours a day; what is the pleasure? The answer is that I don't do it for the pleasure. I do it for the pain. In my most painful moments on the bike, I am at my most self-aware and self-defining. There is a point in every race when a rider encounters the real opponent and realizes that it's...himself. You might say pain is my chosen way of exploring the human heart."

My Ironman races were never about qualifying for Hawaii. That was Big League, usually an hour or more faster than my finish times. Kona was out of reach, but I was more than happy to race Ironman for those moments of self-awareness and exploration.

But things began to change last Fall, when I began breaking personal barriers. Three sub-3 hour marathons (including a 2:54 at Boston 2002), and a 19th place AG finish at Ironman New Zealand 2002 (20 minutes from a Kona slot) indicated I was in new territory as an athlete, and maybe, just maybe, ready to try to earn entry to The Ironman World Championships at Kona.

I approached this Ironman much differently than previous races. I dramatically shifted training time from the run to the bike, and stepped up the hours from an average of seven per week to nearly ten hours. I felt more ready than ever by mid-July.

I had raced Ironman USA in 1999, and finished in 12:22. I arrived in Lake Placid aiming to finish below the 10:42 time that earned the last Kona slot in my M40-44 age group in 2001.

Swim

I always have a single goal in the swim – exit the water fresh, so I could take advantage of my better events – and this race would be no different. Temperatures were in the high 50s as the cannon fired at 7am, starting the race for 1754 contestants.

Despite the congestion in tiny Mirror Lake, the contact at the start was minimal, and I stayed away from aggressive action by swimming wide. I just tried to swim straight. Timing data supplied by Marc Roy of Sportstats, shows that I was 794th to complete lap 1 of the swim, typical of recent efforts.

On lap 2, I think I followed the same person the entire way, buoy to buoy, and interestingly, exited the water in 793rd place in 1:10. You don't get more consistent than that.

The run to Transition 1 is about ¼ mile, I ran fast to shave time, and it worked. At 0:05:31, my T1 was 306th fastest, and if the data is correct, I passed 97 people in the transition area on the way to the bike start.

Bike

My shift to bike emphasis was obvious in this year's training log – I averaged 30 miles per week in 2001, but was up to 85 miles per week in 2002, with several 150+ mile weeks. These totals are low compared to most fast riders, but they gave me the confidence that I would significantly improve on the 6:35 bike time I posted at Ironman USA in 1999.

The Ironman USA bike course is technical, with continuous rolling and turning terrain, and an elevation change of 7624 feet over two 56 mile laps. My bike strategy was probably too simple: ride in control, maintain high cadence where possible, and don't implode on the last ten climbing miles.

Once on the bike, I rode based on feel, and I felt aggressive. I just wanted to attack. Out of the saddle on the crests of hills, I drove past other riders. They may have thought I was crazy, but most weren't able to catch me to let me know.

I finished lap 1 feeling strong, with a time of 2:41:29, or about 20.8 mph. Data for the first 56 miles was uploaded to the Internet on www.ironmanlive.com. Friends, including Joe Foster, multiple-time Kona qualifier and my race advisor, were watching. With the live data, they knew far more than I did about what was happening, including that I had the 204th fastest bike split for the lap.

After seeing the lap 1 results, Joe sent an email to several Iron friends, saying:

"Based on a very quick scan of the top 60 (M40-44) at the 'half bike' posting, only 25 seem to have a pace that is interesting. Key for Ray (at about 57th M40-44 and moving up) will be holding his pace against the tide of deterioration that will sweep the field after the 'lap of exuberance' is done and reality sets in (Lap 1.5-2). He must be feeding off the energy of all those racers he is passing as he moves up the field!"

Things got interesting just after lap 2 began, as it started to rain. Wet road and this course don't mix well, and that meant all riders had to slow down. That didn't prevent bloody crashes, which led me to ride even more cautiously as the rain began pounding harder and harder. But I had energy to spare, and had no problem powering through the hard climbs between mile 101 and 111.

Part of my energy reserve came from having the right gearing. I had obsessed before the race about which cassette to use – a 12-23 for speed, or 12-25 to better manage the climbs. Never the shy one, my brother-in-law called his friend George Hincapie (Lance Armstrong's lieutenant on Team US Postal), at the Tour de France, to pose the question. The reply from Hincapie, shortly after his epic pull during Stage 11 in the Pyrenees: "Go with the 12x25. I have never heard of anyone regretting having one more gear."

He was right. There is nothing like the feeling of having climbed 7600 feet on the bike over 111 miles, and feeling more ready than ever to run a marathon.

With the rain, my pace did deteriorate on lap 2, but the same was true for just about everyone. I finished with the 276th fastest lap 2, for 246th best bike time overall at 5:41:37. This was my best bike positioning ever, and I had passed 288 racers along the way.

Run

After a 49th fastest T2 overall in 0:02:13, I sprinted (not an exaggeration) onto the run course in 308th place.

With the lap 2 bike data in hand from www.ironmanlive.com, Joe emailed the group again as I started running:

"Ray is off the bike in 47th M40-44 position! VERY promising is the fact that he is near dead-on his time goals and his T-2 was *very* fast.

From 'cyber-land,' this indicates that he is executing on his race plan and taking free time from his lesser competitors.

"My forecast: Ray gets 13/14 positions on the basis of attrition (fast swimmers on the decline, poor second bike laps and assumptions based on long T-2s). He will need to throw everything into the run to battle it out with the remaining 33 racers."

That's exactly what I did. The 2:54 at Boston in April finally convinced me that I'm a Real Runner. I tore into the run telling myself that there were few who could run better, and I planned to prove it.

The two-lap run course is among the more challenging on the Ironman circuit, with steep climbs on two sections, and other twists and turns. The cool rain ended as my run began, and the sun came out, for a dramatic heat increase, impacting body temperature regulation for all competitors.

The first 13 miles were a blur of spotting the next guy, checking to see if he was in my age group, passing him, repeat. At the turnarounds, I checked to see how many in my age group were ahead, and the numbers weren't significant. I kept picking M40-44s off one at a time, and rarely was anyone able to hold my pace for long.

My worst period was between miles 14 and 20, when it seems my systems were out of balance. Art Hutchinson, Ironman veteran, was spectating, and noted I was both flush in the face, and had goosebumps on my arms. My vision was going blurry, and for a few minutes I thought I was in trouble. I began devouring cola, Gatorade and oranges at aid stations, and felt somewhat better. The good news was, I was still passing people, but my pace had slowed.

I only checked my watch at the mile 21 point, and saw 9:50 had elapsed. With 5.2 miles to go, I would have to dig in to finish comfortably within last year's qualifying time of 10:42. I picked up the pace, and drove myself back into town, continuing the drop the occasional M40-44 athlete who had surrendered to the heat. Former Ironman Canada winner Michael McCormack once told me his Ironman mantra: as the race goes longer, I get stronger. At this point, I knew what he meant.

I saw Art at mile 24, he shouted 'it's yours if you want it! Run!' I turned up the speed and motored toward the finish. On the last mile, I spotted a group of several runners well in front of me. Too far ahead, I thought. To my surprise, I caught all but one.

With great happiness, exhaustion and relief, I ran into the finish area on the 400-meter speedskating Olympic Oval, having passed 198 runners on the marathon course, including 34 in my age group. My 3:33 marathon was 55th fastest of the day, and a PR by 6 minutes. At 10:33:51, I finished 13th M40-44, and ultimately, about 15 minutes ahead of the last qualifying finisher.

The next day, I collected my Kona slot.

As each day goes by, I'm increasingly overwhelmed by what this achievement means. I never dreamed that running a 4:41 Chicago Marathon in October 1994 would begin an endurance racing career that would lead me on an eventual path to Kona. It's been an amazing journey.

Vineman Ironman 1997 11:34:06
Ironman Canada 1997 11:47:40
Ironman Europe 1998 11:40:31
Ironman Switzerland 1998 12:46:07
Ironman Canada 1998 12:42:27
Ironman New Zealand 1999 12:08:04
Ironman USA 1999 12:22:38
Ironman Canada 1999 11:59:36
Ironman Florida 1999 11:15:57
Ironman California 2000 13:35:23
Ironman Florida 2000 11:09:40
Ironman Austria 2001 11:26:55
Ironman Florida 2001 10:40:13
Ironman New Zealand 2002 10:41:58
Ironman USA 2002 10:33:51

What's made the difference in performance? In short: increased biking/less running, more high intensity workouts, increased training time overall, stronger/leaner physique, and strong mental determination.

Kona Slot #2: Ironman Wisconsin 2002

Immediately after the announcement of Ironman Wisconsin in the summer of 2001, I signed up to be part of the inaugural event, much as I had done three years earlier upon the announcement of the first Ironman USA in Lake Placid. I booked the race in my calendar, and went on my way trying to improve my Ironman performance at other races.

In November 2001, I finished Ironman Florida in 10:40, about 40 minutes from a Kona slot. Four months later in New Zealand, a 10:41 finish in wind and rain was about 20 minutes short of Kona. In July, it all came together in a 10:33 at Lake Placid, and my goal had been reached: Kona 2002.

I found myself at the Ironman Wisconsin start line at 7am on Sunday September 15 with an unexpected opportunity and challenge: qualify for Kona for the second time in seven weeks, this time for the 2003 race. I wasn't sure I was up to it.

In my pre race notes, I wrote:

" . . . frankly, after going all out in Lake Placid, and more recently at Mrs. T's, and just coming off an 8-day, very low training volume vacation, I wonder if my heart will be completely in it. The fire is returning, but will it be there September 15? Does it need to be?

"Worst case, it's a fun, long training day, close to home. Best case, though, it's a run at qualifying for Hawaii, 2003. This is the first qualifier for the 2003 race, which probably stacks the deck a bit against me. There are only 80 overall slots available, compared with 100 at Lake Placid, meaning that my age group might receive only 8 or 9 slots. Second, I assume I'll have to finish in the top 8 or 9 to get a slot; I anticipate no rolldown, since this is the first event of the year. Last, I will race hard, but, yes, I am mindful that Hawaii will be five weeks away, and will back off if and when necessary. "

Joe Foster, my Ironman training advisor, sensed my ambivalence, and let me have it two days before the race. To paraphrase, he said: 'if you're going to jeopardize a good performance five weeks later in Kona -- and you are by doing this race -- the pressure is on you to deliver; you've got a job to do; you need to qualify for Kona 2003, that must be your goal'.

It seemed a little harsh at the time. I tried to find ways to let myself off the hook, but I had to admit he was right: I had a job to do.

When I finished the race, the first question people asked me was: do you think you qualified? I didn't know. Second question: how does this race compare with Ironman USA Lake Placid? (which I had finished weeks earlier) That, I knew.

Both are great races, and I recommend each highly. I rate the courses as nearly equally challenging overall, but they are quite different in many obvious ways.

For starters, Ironman USA is set in the 1980 US Winter Olympic site of Lake Placid, a small town nestled in the Adirondack mountains, while Ironman Wisconsin is set in the heart of Wisconsin's state capitol, Madison, home of University of Wisconsin and its 40,000 students, surrounded by farming communities.

Madison, Wisconsin opened its arms and embraced this inaugural race in impressive fashion. The people were overwhelmingly friendly and supportive. The course wound through scenic farmland, through the university and with the state capitol building as the backdrop to the finish line. A photo-op race, if I've ever been in one.

The similarities begin and end with the swim. Both are two loop, rectangular courses in fresh water (although that term is less applicable to zero visibility Lake Monona than to Lake Placid's Mirror Lake).

Swim

At 7am in Madison, more than 1800 athletes took off to complete the two-rectangle loop swim in Lake Monona, in front of Monona Terrace convention hall, a unique structure inspired by Frank Lloyd Wright.

I expected a typical 1:10 swim, which I achieved in Lake Placid, but didn't get it in Madison.

The swim seemed more unpleasant than usual. I've never had so much contact in an Ironman swim. My favorite goggles developed a streaming leak after 400 meters. Some sort of current and/or my lousy navigating pulled me off course a few times. I kept running into people and having to stop and start again.

Approaching the clock at the end, I had no idea what it would read. But seeing 1:15:29, my heart sank. My worst swim in two years. Not a complete surprise, given the struggles in the water, but very disappointing.

Swim times were slower by several minutes for many racers. Of course I didn't know that until *after* the race, so for a while I was beating myself up for being such a lousy swimmer (actual thought: either quit triathlon or learn how to swim much, much better!).

I was smack in the middle of the pack, 873rd, compared to 792nd out of the water in Lake Placid. I thought I was out of Kona contention from the start. But I tried to remember Joe Foster's advice after a similar experience in Hawaii: never let the swim time distract you from the job at hand.

So off I went, to the most convoluted transition area in Ironman history. In Lake Placid, transition is fairly typical: run out of the water to the Olympic Speed Skating oval, to change and grab your bike and go.

In Madison, there was no such open area for a normal transition; instead the Monona Terrace building was the transition area. Picture this: run up four levels of a circular parking ramp (affectionately called 'the helix' by race officials) to the upper level parking garage, to the middle of the level, then inside (!) into a big Monona Terrace conference room to pick up your bag and to change.

Then out the door, run fifty yards to bike entry, and scamper approximately a hundred yards to bike exit, which was a fun trip riding *down* the other side helix to ground level. It was amazing, and it took me and most people more than eight minutes to do it all.

After the transition area, in the first 1/4 mile of the bike on John Nolen Drive, there was a narrow path and a big bump I could not avoid. Bam! 4 PowerBars flew off my bike. No room to stop and fetch them, I kept going, with 920 fewer calories for the bike course than I needed.

All-in-all, not a good first 85 minutes in Madison. I wondered if it was my time for a 'bad day.' I had not fully recovered from Ironman USA, and I really didn't train for this race. I was so focused on Ironman

USA, and had all training aimed at it, that when I was there, I wanted to explode. In Madison, it wasn't happening . . . yet.

Bike

I saw the Ironman Wisconsin bike course for the first time only the day before the race, and finally understood what people had been telling me for weeks: the course is unending turns and climbs. Some people who had trained on both courses had described the Madison course as harder than Lake Placid.

This surprised me, until I rode it. The elevation chart showed that these climbs took place within a range or 840 and 1240 feet above sea level, so no climb exceeded 400 feet at one time. That seemed reasonable, compared with 1500 foot climbs at Lake Placid. At least on paper.

But the difference between the two courses is simple: Lake Placid's climbs are long and arduous; Wisconsin's climbs hit you again and again.

Wisconsin's bike course is two loops, but the 40-mile loops began 16 miles from town. Lake Placid is two 56 mile loops. Winds seemed fairly strong out of the northwest in Madison, and were a constant test all day. But the sun remained out all day, unlike the downpour we got in Lake Placid.

Lake Placid's first seven miles are mainly up at 12mph, the next seven miles are straight down at 40+mph. A fairly flat few miles follow to the town of Jay, then riders work their way uphill back to Lake Placid. The most challenging aspect of the Lake Placid course is the 10-mile climb past Whiteface Mountain that begins at mile approximately 45 and 101. (More detail can be found in my Ironman USA xtri.com report.)

By contrast, the first leg of IM WI gently rolls along the countryside, getting you warmed up, and thankfully, there were no long climbs. Nothing seemed to exceed half a mile in duration. But they came one after the other, all day.

The Madison course runs mostly through Wisconsin's farmland, with just a few miles through local communities. Highlights were the extreme rollercoaster hills on Witte Road and beyond, passing through a cow path on North Birch trail to approach the toughest hill of the day, getting Gatorade from SuperWoman at the superhero aid station after mile 50/90, and blasting through crowds of people lining the road Tour de France-style, in Verona.

Passing through Verona at mile 55 was awesome, then we headed back west to begin the next 40 miles of the second loop. Through that point, I my confidence was building. I was riding fast, passing strong riders, and feeling more and more certain I could offset the poor swim if I kept up the pace.

By mile 60, though, I was beginning to feel noticeably sore and slow. I'm prepared for at least one bad portion on the bike; this was it. Doubts began creeping in again -- had I not recovered enough from Lake Placid? Would I recover in time for the hills on Witte Road and beyond? But you keep going, drink Gatorade, eat, and try to keep the cadence up. At mile 75, I felt myself again. Thank goodness.

The second loop finished, we headed back towards Madison, but not before a final climb to mile 105. The winds had picked up with more intensity, and speeds began to sag. At this point, I looked at my watch for the first time in more than 5 hours, and it said 6:40 had elapsed. After the slow swim, long T1, and a hilly course, I had a chance to arrive near the 7 hour point, not far off what I had done in Lake Placid.

I hammered back into town, and back up the helix to transition 2, as the clock read 7:02. I had finished the ride in 5:37:58, passing 607 riders, more than 1/3 of the field, to have the 157th best ride on the day. This was my best cycling rank ever, ahead of 244th in Lake Placid. Maybe I could salvage this race after all.

Run

The run course was filled with climbs, just like the bike course. I wasn't excited about it, but I knew it was more likely to tear down others, and I could use it to my advantage. As I exited transition 2 uphill towards the state Capitol, I knew if I were to have any chance at Kona, I'd have to make the run count.

The course elevation map shows 13 climbs of about 100 feet each, making this the most challenging Ironman run course I'd experienced. The Lake Placid course features two sharp hills at one and three miles

into each run loop, the second of which was a long, half mile monster.
But the rest of the Lake Placid course seemed flat.

In Madison, the run out of T2 goes directly uphill to the Capitol. After
the capitol, the course heads out west through (nice touch!) Camp
Randall, the Badger's football stadium, to an out-and-back on
Observatory Drive through campus, and State Street, another out-and-
back loop on the bike trail, then back to the capitol via the football
stadium. I really liked this layout; always something different.

I had planned to check my watch to keep on pace, but I couldn't read
it. I was too foggy. So I just ran as fast as I felt I could. My Kona
hopes seemed diminished as I saw several in my age group returning
to town as I was headed out, clearly far ahead.

I knew I needed to be top 10 in my age group (M40-44) to have any
chance at a slot, and assumed there were many between me and the
front-runners. But the beauty of the course is that you get four chances
each look to scan who's ahead of you, at the turnarounds. Surprisingly,
I didn't see that many in my age group. Was there a chance?

I reached the 13.1 mile turnaround at the Capitol, and looked closely
at my watch for the first time since the run began. Not bad: 1:45 for
13.1 miles, and I felt fine.

I never had a bad moment on the run, perhaps because I kept eating.
Having lost the Powerbars on the bike several hours earlier, I was
concerned I'd run out of energy, so I took GU every 4 miles. I do this
automatically in stand-alone marathons, but had never tried it in
Ironman. It seemed to work.

I started recognizing people in my age group getting closer to me at
the turnarounds, and passing the occasional one. Two things kept me
on my toes: neighbor, training partner, and Iron rookie Barry
Schliesmann was nearly exactly on my pace, about 4 minutes back,
and #1338 also seemed to be eyeing me, trying to narrow the gap.
They gave me a new motivation -- stay ahead. Each turnaround I
checked, and each time they were still there.

I saw fewer and fewer male 40-44 runners on the last turnaround at
mile 23, and started thinking -- without any real basis to do so -- that
maybe I could go top 10. I had finished 13th in M40-44 at Lake
Placid; maybe this could be a personal best ranking.

The key moment for me occurred on University Street, during mile 24. I spotted two M40-44 runners ahead of me, guys I knew were contenders. I knew they would not let me pass easily, being this close to the finish, and possibly close to a Kona slot.

I learned a lesson in Lake Placid, when I unsuccessfully tried to pass a final strong M40-44 runner near the end. I passed, he remained on my shoulder, and I couldn't shake him. When we were 50 yards from the finish, he pulled outside and outsprinted me to the finish. I couldn't answer.

In Madison, I didn't want to repeat this scenario. I needed to drop these two decisively, and waited until another runner passed them, hopefully distracting them, to make my move. I passed with as much sustained speed as possible, looked for shadows -- the sun was from the rear, and would outline anyone nearby -- and saw none. For the remaining two miles, I ran from the shadows (ultimately, I got three minutes ahead of them).

Running confidently, but on fumes -- I had no feeling in my hands or feet -- I passed the Capitol one final time, and headed for the finish. The clock showed 10:42:49 and 139th place and for the first time all day, I knew I had done well. I had passed 126 runners on the marathon.

I emerged from medical more than two hours later, in the dark, and returned to the finish line to see friend and training partner John Mueting finish his second Ironman with a smile. Then I looked on the results pages posted there, and saw what I had sensed: 10th place in my age group. My best Ironman age group rank at that point in time.

The next day, I collected my Kona 2003 slot.

Kona 2002: Debut

'How long have you been preparing for the race?'

It's a question I heard from several curious strangers on our trip from Kona back to Chicago, two days after finishing the 2002 Ironman Triathlon World Championship. I hadn't really acknowledged it until asked, but the answer was simple.

Every triathlete has their moment when they know they have to do the Hawaii Ironman. For me, it was the final minutes of NBC's broadcast of the 1994 Ironman that did it. In the last few minutes of the show, after the winners had come in, with Thomas Newman's 'Little Women' soundtrack tugging on emotions, I watched athlete after athlete cross the finish line in Kona in various forms of elation and/or exhaustion. Some jumped for joy, others collapsed. After 140.6 challenging swim/bike/run miles, they had finished the Ironman, and that was supremely special.

Those televised finishes gripped me in an unexplainable way; ask any triathlete, and they know what I mean. I just had to do it. Nearly eight years later, after qualifying at Ironman USA Lake Placid, I finally had my chance to join the finishers.

Pre-race

In the previous twelve months, I had gone into races to compete, to beat people, to place highly, to qualify. The strange thing in Kona was, there would be none of that. I was now surrounded by the best of the best. And most of them had been to Kona before. I knew that the race would be humbling.

But it didn't matter. I was there, finally. Under drizzly, overcast skies, at 7am on Saturday October 19, the cannon went off, and all of a sudden, I was in the middle of a dream. I was in the middle of the Ironman Triathlon World Championship.

But the difference between a dream and this moment was simple: I still needed to swim 2.4 miles, bike 112 miles and run a marathon of 26.2 miles to realize the goal. There was work to do. Your don't collect your reward until you finish.

Swim

Knowing I was among a field of great swimmers, I seeded myself a few yards behind the line. This swim was without a wetsuit, which I knew would cost me some time, and as usual, I did not plan to push hard on the swim. I had told friends to expect me out of the water in 1:20:00.

The ocean swells had been invading the swim course for the previous day, and had not abated for the race. Shortly after passing the pier, we were in the middle of it. I was getting tossed around continuously, and rarely saw the buoys. I just kept my head down, and followed people in front of me, assuming they knew where they were going. Generally they did.

By the ¾ mile point, my goggles were blurry, but I swore I saw whitecaps. I ignored the thought during the swim, but the photo confirms it: we were riding the breaks.

Despite the turbulence, I felt pretty comfortable in the water. Given the conditions, I was pleased to see 1:18:57 on the clock when I finished, a minute or so ahead of schedule.

Out of the water into Transition 1, run through the hoses to wash some salt water off, grab your bag, into the changing tent, get cycling clothes and shoes on, grab your bike, and go. And the crowds were huge exiting transition, and heading up Palani Road. Into the rain.

Bike

The 112 mile Kona bike course is legendary for it's endless miles through inferno-like lava fields and occasionally furious winds. And they didn't disappoint.

The first few miles weave in and around Kailua-Kona, before heading north on the Queen K highway through the lava fields. It rained for the first hour, but that kept conditions cool, and we had what seemed like a tailwind out of town. I passed through the first 30 miles in 20.4 mph, feeling great.

I had heard over and over about the winds on the climb to Hawi, and was repeatedly urged not to fight them too hard. The winds were there as expected, and the sun was out and hot, while I covered the next 30 miles to the apex of the bike course in Hawi, averaging 17.9 mph.

I had also heard that after dealing with headwinds for more than an hour, the tailwind after the turnaround would be short-lived, followed by shifting cross-winds off the volcano. Those cross winds make the screaming downhill a sometimes nerve-wracking experience. I covered this third leg of 30 miles in 21.3 mph.

After all this, I reached mile 90 in just under 20mph pace. Thoughts about a possible 5:45 bike finish were quickly dashed as headwinds slowed me to 15mph for the final 22 miles. But for the first time, I began thinking about the run. My legs felt fine, and I chose not to fight the winds in these final miles, in order to have that energy for the marathon ahead.

I had told friends to expect a 6:15:00 bike ride, given conditions, but I wheeled in with a faster 6:01:54. Still, I wondered if I should have done better.

Run

After a quick shoe change in Transition 2, I headed out in the bright sun to run the marathon. The course departs transition generally south through town to an Alii Drive out and back. The 3 mile point passed our hotel, but I got there ahead of expectation and my family wasn't there. That was fine, I was feeling poorly, a rare feeling for me in the marathon. Still, I made it to the 5.5 mile turn at an 8:03/mile pace, though I'm not really sure where that speed came from.

Returning north on Alii, the family was waiting as I passed 8 miles. I stopped to kiss and hug the kids, and told Wendy I'd be finishing earlier than the 6:45pm arrival I originally told her to expect. 'Be at the finish area at 6:15, and I'll probably finish by 6:30pm,' I said. Then I took off.

As the course wound back up to the lava fields on the Queen K, I kept feeling stronger. Also, very overheated. It was getting excruciatingly hot. I ran with ice in my cap, and wet sponges in my shirt from mile to mile, but kept feeling faster. The downside of all the sweat and fluid is blisters form easily. Both feet were soon burning from more than the heat.

Turning into the legendary Energy Lab segment – miles 15 to 20 – I knew this was the place where races were made or broken. This is where my monthly solo marathon training runs come into play – when the mind must overcome physical aches and pains. I stuck to my plan, and kept passing people, while seeing others give in.

Out of the Energy Lab still feeling fine, there were three runners who kept playing cat and mouse with me. At different times, each would pass, then slow to walk, and I passed them back, eventually for good. It helped get through the final miles approaching Kailua-Kona. And it was fun to think to myself: I ran the Chicago Marathon in 3:05 six days ago, and I'm still passing these folks. I passed 270 runners, nearly 20% of the finishers, in the marathon.

Kona veterans say the final stretch north on Alii Drive is magical and they are right. I was advised to soak it in and enjoy. I don't usually react to crowds, preferring to stay focused until the end, but this was special. I broke form and was high-fiving outstretched hands. Next thing I knew, several of those hands were those of my family, who had arrived there at 6:15, as I suggested.

I glanced up at the clock, just a few yards ahead, and saw I was right on time. In the noise and the lights, I crossed the line at 6:17pm, for an 11:17:21 Ironman finish.

I'm very happy with this first finish at Ironman, but I'll be faster next year when I return for the 2003 race.

'How long have you been preparing for this race?' the curious will again ask afterwards next year. I'll reply: I never stop preparing.

Returning to Kona

- Qualifying Training Plan Strategy Year 2
- Kona Slot #3: Ironman Wisconsin 2003
- Kona 2003: Racing the Sunset
- Qualifying Training Strategy 2003

Qualifying Training Plan Strategy Year 2

Ever think you don't train enough to compete effectively? It's easy to feel that way. According to the official Ironman website: "The average Ironman triathlete spends 18 to 24 hours each week training for this event. A typical week includes seven miles of swimming, 225 miles of biking and 48 miles of running." Who has that kind of time? Not me.

I know I'm not alone trying to get the most out of limited training time. Most age group triathletes have to fit this fun little hobby around everything else that goes along with normal life. We do the best we can with the time we have. Which is probably why the most common question I got from www.xtri.com readers in 2003 was: how much do you train, and when?

The 'when' is easy. As a 43-year-old telecom executive helping to raise four children aged 5 to 14, most of my training occurs when most people are asleep, either early in the morning or late at night. Summer weekend mornings tend to be the exceptions, when my wife graciously gives me the opportunity to do long rides through mid-morning.

The answer to 'how much do you train'? Naturally it varies throughout the year, but I averaged training about 7.5 hours per week in 2003, about an hour less than in 2002.

Even though those numbers are significantly below the reported qualifier averages, I still had a solid season, including a 2:55 marathon and qualifying for Kona 2004. But the season had a rocky start.

1994 to 2003 Training Mileage and Time Summary

Mileage	Swim	Bike	Run	Total
1994	-	-	150.0	150.0
1995	12.3	290.0	1,251.1	1,553.4
1996	43.6	925.7	1,624.8	2,594.1
1997	68.9	1,781.5	1,206.0	3,056.5
1998	38.2	2,667.9	1,097.2	3,803.3
1999	27.4	2,276.1	1,198.7	3,502.2
2000	15.3	1,525.8	1,387.3	2,928.4
2001	103.5	2,463.6	1,522.1	4,089.2
2002	146.3	3,830.8	1,347.7	5,324.8
2003	83.7	3,577.8	1,372.0	5,033.5
Total	539.2	19,339.1	12,157.1	32,035.4

Hours	Swim	Bike	Run	Total
1994	0:00:00	0:00:00	21:52:30	21:52:30
1995	7:38:37	17:24:14	168:33:04	193:35:54
1996	27:10:57	55:33:16	205:10:19	287:54:32
1997	39:41:19	101:38:28	165:48:34	307:08:21
1998	21:36:45	147:32:39	147:12:06	316:21:30
1999	14:45:01	119:14:11	175:21:31	309:20:43
2000	9:03:52	85:49:19	184:41:38	279:34:49
2001	57:36:28	130:40:23	187:16:16	375:33:07
2002	78:27:19	196:47:00	167:55:26	443:09:45
2003	44:19:34	179:58:59	168:06:27	392:25:00
Total	300:19:52	1034:38:29	1591:57:51	2926:56:12

A Bad Start

Here's my 2003 story. It started with high expectations, after a breakthrough season full of personal bests in 2002. As I wrote in my 'Deconstructing 2002' column a year ago, the breakthrough came from a big jump in my training from 7.25 weekly training hours in 2001 to 8.5 training hours in 2002. My big increase had been more time on the bike, and I was convinced that was the key to qualifying for Kona my first time in 2002.

So as I made 2003 plans, I expected to train more and do better. Simple. Until I tripped over an unexpected obstacle on a night run (the downside of training when everyone else sleeps!), injuring my knee and shoulder. I had been hoping to begin the year with big training hours, but instead spent months trying to negotiate a recovery with my body, which only let me reach a 9-hour training week once in the first four months of the year.

Even though my key triathlon – Ironman Wisconsin – was not until September, I had geared my entire race season to build to that event, with at least one major race per month starting in March. Solid performances in those early races had built confidence and laid the foundation for even better races in 2002.

Having to deal with nagging knee, calf, hamstring and shoulder injuries through spring, my hopes for speed were replaced by endless training frustrations. Through the first 17 weeks of 2003, I was only able to average 6 hours per week training, more than half of that on the run. During this period I averaged less than two hours per week on the bike and less than an hour in the water. My first fitness test was the March Madness Half Marathon during week 12. Calf spasms had me walking during later miles, and

2003 Training Summary: Weekly Training Time Chart

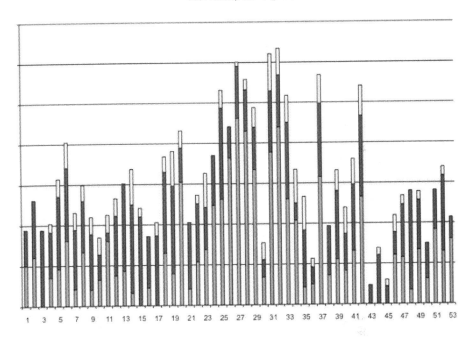

2003 Weekly Training Time

sorely (in more ways than one) concerned about the season.

Though I had expected to reach a peak in April, hopes for a 2:55 marathon were replaced by a disappointing 3:06 Boston. While I reached sub-3 hour marathon territory in May, at that point my cycling was far behind expectations, and my training log noted that I struggled through a 68 mile ride on May 17. Things did not look good, and I was worried.

Turning it all Around

But it all started to come together in mid-June. Was it the forced downtime in the early part of the season? I didn't know, but suddenly my rides began exceeding 20 mph, my runs felt more together, and it seemed to be coming back. Finally injury free, I was able to transition to 4-week cycles of increasingly more time and distance per week.

My training time from weeks 18 to 34 jumped to an average 10:12 per week: 6 hours on the bike, 3 hours running and 1 hour swimming. I still was as time-constrained as ever, but with the sun rising at near 5am during this period, I was often able to get up to 2 hours training before having breakfast, driving the kids to school and heading into work.

Key to improved performance during this period was an internal challenge I set for myself: do a long ride of 80 to 100 miles every week, if possible. Start Saturday morning before the sun rises, regardless of the weather, and just do it. And for the first time ever, I was logging more than 200 weekly cycling miles on a regular basis. It helped bring me almost back to 2002 shape, even though my total training time still lagged.

During this period I tried to follow a simple menu of workouts:

- Two swim workouts (light, but my shoulder was still hurting)
- One 9 mile speed workout run
- Two 9 to 13 mile recovery runs
- One 'time trial' 30 to 45 mile bike ride (target 22mph)
- One 30-45 mile ride a notch or two below time trial (21mph)
- One 80 to 100 mile ride
- Where possible, add short brick runs on to bike rides

2003 Totals

Data	Bike	Run	Swim	Grand Total
Sum of Distance	3,577.80	1,372.04	83.66	5,033.50
Sum of Time	179:58:59	168:06:27	44:19:34	392:25:00
Count of Type	131	139	81	351
Avg Dist/Exercise	27.31	9.87	1.03	14.34
Avg Time/Exercise	1:22:26	1:12:34	0:32:50	1:07:05
Avg Time/mile	03:01.1	07:21.1	31:47.4	04:40.7
Time/day	0:29:40	0:27:43	0:07:18	1:04:41
Time/week	3:27:40	3:13:58	0:51:09	7:32:47
Dist/week	68.80	26.39	1.61	96.80

Major Races	Date	Time
Boston Marathon	April	3:06:01
MadCity Marathon	May	2:59:58
Ironman USA Lake Placid	July	10:49:06
Lake Zurich Olympic Distance	August	2:05:47
Chicago Triathlon	August	2:15:27
Ironman Wisconsin	September	10:38:24
Milwaukee Marathon	October	2:55:28
Ironman World Championship	October	10:55:27

Peaking

By August, it all came together with a 6th place age group finish at the Chicago Triathlon, followed two weeks later by a 6th place age group finish and a Kona 2004 slot at Ironman Wisconsin. Both were my best triathlon finish ranks ever. Though biking was my priority all summer, I still felt like I had a fast marathon in me, and it came out in the form of a 2:55:26, also 6th in my age group, at the Milwaukee Lakefront Marathon in October. And to cap it all off, I knocked 22 minutes off my best time at Kona, finishing in 10:55:27.

Moral of the story: you may have several months where you're falling below expectations due to injury or other reasons, and you can still come back and finish strong.

What was surprising to me when I looked at the weekly detail is that while I was in peak racing form after week 35, when I wasn't racing, my training time was significantly reduced, primarily for either taper or recovery from these major races. During weeks 35 to 52, which admittedly include big declines in activity post-Kona, weekly averages dropped back to the 6-hour level.

2003 Training Summary: Weekly Time

Weekly Time

Sum of Time	Type			
Week	Bike	Run	Swim	Grand Total
1	2:26:00	2:05:57		4:31:57
2	2:54:45	3:22:51		6:17:36
3		4:30:50		4:30:50
4	1:41:00	2:42:18	0:30:27	4:53:45
5	2:12:49	4:17:30	1:01:52	7:32:11
6	3:52:49	4:19:14	1:30:47	9:42:50
7	1:00:00	3:31:05	1:01:10	5:32:15
8	3:11:57	3:02:03	0:56:11	7:10:11
9	0:57:36	3:17:44	1:00:31	5:15:51
10	1:33:33	1:29:13	1:00:48	4:03:34
11	3:51:09	0:29:45	1:03:07	5:24:01
12	1:48:02	3:32:04	1:02:32	6:22:38
13	2:04:30	5:10:25		7:14:55
14	0:45:00	5:15:16	2:06:02	8:06:18
15		5:16:49	0:31:20	5:48:09
16	1:03:08	3:03:28		4:06:36
17		4:09:01	0:47:32	4:56:33
18	3:06:50	4:47:42	0:55:22	8:49:54
19	1:53:50	5:11:19	2:03:20	9:08:29
20	7:19:23	2:00:59	1:01:35	10:21:57
21	0:58:45	3:56:21		4:55:06
22	2:34:54	3:27:07	0:30:20	6:32:21
23	3:18:41	2:30:28	2:00:56	7:50:05
24	5:56:27	2:56:25		8:52:52
25	6:17:53	5:23:21	1:03:56	12:45:10
26	8:43:31	1:51:42		10:35:13
27	11:04:54	3:05:30	0:15:00	14:25:24
28	10:19:28	2:26:11	0:37:35	13:23:14
29	8:01:01	2:31:33	1:10:10	11:42:44
30	1:39:36	1:01:11	1:00:30	3:41:17
31	9:03:50	3:37:21	2:13:06	14:54:17
32	10:33:31	3:04:27	1:35:29	15:13:27
33	6:16:33	4:32:08	1:36:34	12:25:15
34	5:00:11	1:00:47	2:00:20	8:01:18
35	1:02:19	3:21:29	2:00:24	6:24:12
36	1:12:35	0:59:39	0:31:10	2:43:24
37	7:34:40	4:21:20	1:41:32	13:37:32
38	1:44:10	2:54:29		4:38:39
39	2:41:41	4:02:40	1:13:09	7:57:30
40	2:00:00	2:10:25	1:34:45	5:45:10
41	3:10:24	3:55:46	1:31:22	8:37:32
42	6:23:18	4:47:43	1:47:16	12:58:17
43		1:06:57		1:06:57
44		2:54:34	0:25:00	3:19:34
45		1:02:27	0:24:02	1:26:29
46	2:55:23	1:19:28	1:00:55	5:15:46
47	2:46:52	3:07:21	0:31:45	6:25:58
48	0:50:00	5:53:24		6:43:24
49	3:13:08	2:56:38	0:30:11	6:39:57
50	1:30:03	2:05:18		3:35:21
51	4:24:48	2:20:15		6:45:03
52	3:07:17	4:29:14	0:31:31	8:08:02
53	3:50:45	1:17:15		5:08:00
Grand Total	179:58:59	168:06:27	44:19:34	392:25:00

By the Numbers

In 2003, an average training week for me was just 1.61 miles of swimming, 68.80 miles of biking and 26.39 miles of running. Totals for the year:

- Swim: 44 hours, 83 miles; 11% of total training time (2002 totals: 78 hours, 146 miles)
- Bike: 180 hours, 3578 miles; 46% of training time (2002 totals: 197 hours; 3831 miles)
- Run: 168 hours, 1372 miles; 43% of training time (2002 totals: 168 hours, 1347 miles)

Compared with 2002, the differences were immediately obvious. You saw the first one already: running exactly the same amount of hours, but covering 25 more miles in 2003. This was progress! It meant that my average running time per mile dropped from 7:29 to 7:21. Interesting to see how 9 seconds per mile throughout the year can lead to running almost an additional marathon during the course of the season, but it does.

The next thing you'll see is that my swimming was down significantly compared to 2002. This I'll blame on two factors. First, shoulder complications from my mid-winter fall continued to compromise me in the water for months. I rarely swam in the first 12 weeks of the year. Beyond my control. But the bad part is that once the shoulder was healthy, I still didn't aim for more time in the water. This translated into slower Ironman swims. My fault.

2003 Training Summary: Weekly Mileage

Weekly Distance

Sum of Distance	Type			
Week	Bike	Run	Swim	Grand Total
1	48.0	16.5		64.5
2	58.4	26.4		84.8
3		34.9		34.9
4	37.0	21.7	0.9	59.7
5	46.2	32.1	1.9	80.2
6	76.0	34.8	2.8	113.6
7	17.5	28.5	1.9	47.9
8	60.3	25.3	1.7	87.2
9	20.0	24.9	1.9	46.8
10	30.6	12.1	1.9	44.6
11	72.5	4.0	2.0	78.5
12	35.6	30.7	2.0	68.3
13	41.2	44.3		85.5
14	15.8	44.0	4.0	63.8
15		44.5	1.0	45.5
16	20.3	27.1		47.4
17		33.3	1.4	34.7
18	62.6	37.0	1.7	101.3
19	31.9	43.6	3.8	79.3
20	141.8	16.3	1.9	160.0
21	20.0	34.0		54.0
22	50.7	29.3	0.9	80.9
23	62.7	21.9	3.7	88.3
24	118.2	25.4		143.6
25	128.4	45.4	2.0	175.8
26	173.4	15.4		188.8
27	223.4	25.0	0.4	248.8
28	206.0	20.8	1.1	227.9
29	162.3	21.6	2.1	186.0
30	28.9	8.5	1.9	39.3
31	177.6	26.2	4.4	208.2
32	225.7	26.1	3.1	254.9
33	131.4	38.6	3.1	173.0
34	100.4	8.8	3.9	113.1
35	25.0	27.7	3.9	56.6
36	21.5	8.8	1.0	31.3
37	151.1	30.5	3.4	185.0
38	33.0	23.8		56.8
39	54.0	35.0	2.3	91.3
40	41.0	19.4	3.0	63.4
41	62.6	35.0	2.9	100.4
42	122.0	34.7	3.3	160.0
43		8.5		8.5
44		23.1	0.8	23.8
45		8.5	0.8	9.3
46	56.5	9.6	1.9	68.0
47	52.4	23.1	1.0	76.4
48	16.5	49.5		66.0
49	60.0	23.7	0.9	84.6
50	29.5	17.2		46.7
51	90.1	18.9		109.0
52	65.0	36.4	1.0	102.4
53	73.0	9.8		82.8
Grand Total	3,577.8	1,372.0	83.7	5,033.5

Last, my cycling time and mileage was reduced, but most of that difference came in the first few months of the year. In 2002 I had been training for Ironman New Zealand on the CompuTrainer in my basement, and 56 mile rides (or longer) were a weekly staple. In 2003, injuries prevented me from logging as many indoor miles (1243 miles in 2003 vs. 1536 in 2002), and that was the main difference.

The biggest equipment change I made in 2003 was upgrading my bike. I had been thinking about making the jump for a couple of years, but delayed. Most people out there know what this is like: you're riding a bike you're happy with, wondering if it's worth all the expense to get the higher end model if it's going to translate into just a few minutes off your Ironman time.

I was perfectly happy with my Softride PowerWing which I had purchased in 1999 and immediately broke 6 hours for an Ironman bike ride. I had been eyeing a Softride Rocket for two years and finally upgraded in August, hoping I'd see a difference. The improvement was immediate and measurable. During 2003, in training and in races, I covered 1447 miles outdoors on my PowerWing, averaging 19.7 mph. After upgrading to the Rocket, I rode/raced 858 miles on the new bike averaging 20.6 mph. Same effort, 1mph faster. 100 miles training rides averaging 21mph. New territory! A new Ironman bike PR at Ironman Wisconsin. Huge.

Kona Slot #3: Ironman Wisconsin 2003

It had been fifty-one weeks since I qualified for the Ironman Triathlon World Championships in Kona. With Ironman Wisconsin as the first US Kona qualifier for 2004, I wondered if I could do it again. The fitness seemed there, but the track record wasn't quite where I had wanted it to be. Until recent weeks, my race season had been a solid one, but just not quite as good as 2002, and I hadn't had the breakthrough race that I was searching for. Ironman Wisconsin was the key race of the year, and I needed to hit it hard – this was the one that mattered.

As the final days approached, I typed out my vision for the race. I studied it. I internalized the message to the point that when someone would ask for my thoughts on the upcoming race, I'd find myself repeating sections of the typed text verbatim. The words were becoming the game plan for the breakthrough race I had been seeking.

Those words, written two days before the race, began with a sense of realism:

"This Sunday's Ironman is held in and around the university town of Madison Wisconsin. Last year I did not know what to expect, everything started badly, and I fought my way back to earn a Hawaii spot, somewhat to my surprise. This year, I am focused on qualifying for Kona 2004, but also aware that the field is more competitive and it will be a harder task. There are only 9 Kona slots available for the more than 280 competitors in my age group."

While my racing season had been pretty good, 2002 had been better, at least until August. Only my 6th place M40-44 at the Chicago Triathlon two weeks earlier had exceeded 2002 performance. And training levels seemed to be better in August. So the trend was good, but could it carry through to Wisconsin?

Swim

My pre-race words were less than optimistic about the swim, in an effort to prevent the temporary depression that typically sets in after a middle-of-the-pack swim result.

The 2.4 mile swim is a two rectangle loop in Lake Monona, and was terrible for me last year. It was messy, my goggles leaked and fogged up, I went off course, and I exited the water five minutes slower than at Lake Placid. I was supremely unhappy with myself, and that's not a good way to start a 10.5+ hour day. I hope not to repeat the scenario this year, but the swim is my least predictable event. If I can go 1:12:xx as in Lake Placid, I'll be pleased.

At 6:55am, I joined 1810 other athletes in Lake Monona and positioned myself near the front of the pack, but wide right from the crowd. The cannon urged everyone forward at 7:00am, and we were off. This was it . . . time to make things happen! Within the first sixty seconds, in the middle of the congested, churning, frothy water, my heart sank as water began streaming into my goggles. Last year's frustrating swim flashed in front of my eyes, with memories of having to empty my goggles every hundred meters or so. Was it going to happen again?

From the start, it appeared so. I was forced to pull up three times in the first few hundred meters to empty water and try to get a tight seal. Negative thoughts began creeping in, and I quickly searched for something positive: what could possibly be good about this little challenge? Answer: decide that a little running water in the goggles keeps the fog off the lens; hey! I can see the next buoy better! No more going off course! Repeat after me: Stay Positive.

As things began to clear up, I was able to better relax and concentrate on decent form. I was reaching and extending, and it worked. I was also very aware of swimming more efficiently on my side and flowing. Buoy after buoy passed by at what seemed like a good pace. As I swam the northward leg for the final time, catching glances of the Monona Terrace building brimming with spectators at a distance on my left, I began wondering what my swim time might be.

Approaching the swim finish, I felt fast, but I've felt fast before and seen 1:15:xx and hated myself (not really, but you get my point). Squinting at the clock a few meters away, at first all I saw was the 1 and the 8, and honestly thought: it could either be 1:18 or 1:08 and I wouldn't be shocked. What did it say?

When I reached the clock, it said I had reason to be happy: 1:08:54, my second best swim ever, and only 14 seconds short of a personal best. This put me in nearly the top third of racers, 673rd out of 1810 participants. A terrific way to start.

The swim-to-bike transition is the longest and most bizarre in triathlon, going from the beach up a four-story parking garage helix to a top floor transition area inside the Frank Lloyd Wright-designed Monona Terrace building. Then a run of about 150 yards across the whole parking lot to the other side to start the bike. Expect 0:08:30 for transition, hopefully onto the bike course as the clock reads 1:21:xx. If it's slower, it's beyond my control, and I'll have 9+ hours to gain time back.

Highly motivated by an unexpectedly good swim time, I sped through transition hoping to knock a minute or two minutes from last years' T1 time of 0:08:31. The process was a blur, but I do remember entering the bike course with the elapsed time clock reading 1:15:something, about six minutes ahead of my plan. In fact, my transition time was 0:06:28, nearly two minutes better than last year.

Bike

With this great start, I felt in perfect position to execute my bike pre-race bike vision:

"I want to explode on the bike course ('explode' being a relative term, given the distance and the need to preserve for the run), and I would like to shave several minutes compared to last year. I would be thrilled to come in somewhere between 5:28:xx and 5:33:xx, better than 20mph. I will have a carrot to chase; my local training partner — who's very close to me in terms of ability — will probably exit the water about 6-7 minutes before me, and I'll benefit by trying to catch him on the bike (and he'll benefit by trying to stay ahead!)."

I took off in search of speed and my training partner, Barry Schliesmann. In no time, I was flying out of town on John Nolen Drive, picking off riders one by one. The bike course consisted of approximately 17 miles out to a two-loop 39 mile route through beautiful farmland and supportive towns, before retracing the 17 miles back to Monona Terrace. As I passed markers every five miles, I could see I was riding well. I reached 20 miles in 54 minutes, or 22mph. This was great, but I knew the wind and the upcoming hills would bring that speed back to reality. Four miles later, I caught Barry, impossibly early. It turned out we had similar swims, and he had entered the bike course less than two minutes ahead of me. He was also a little tired; he had reason to be.

Barry had delivered a 10:21 at Ironman Canada two weeks earlier. He had also missed his Kona goal by 6 seconds, as he was blocked by a family going through the finish chute, and could only watch helplessly as he was passed by a runner who shot through the family to ultimately take that last slot. The 6-second miss capped a frustratingly star-crossed race season for him, and he was back at Ironman Wisconsin on a mission for Kona 2004. I thought something great was possible for him.

Tired or not, Barry stuck with me, and we soon settled into a well-known scenario. We had done long non-drafting training rides all season, trading the lead every two miles or so. This was the first time we got to try it in a race, and it was great. We flew through the town of Mt. Horeb, roughly mile 30 on the west side of the course, and cruised through the next five miles of roller coaster hills, including the triple threat rollers on Witte Road, still averaging 21.6 mph.

Reaching the north end of the course at mile 40 after some fast descents on Garfoot Road, I felt ok, but I was beginning to have trouble. My right iliotibial band had unexpectedly been tightening up, and would not let go. By mile 45, riding on a narrow road through a farmer's property on Birch Trail, a guy at the side of the road was counting off '. . . 207 . . . 208 . . .' as we rode past. It didn't take long to figure out that he was counting places, and that's where we stood in the race. It seemed like excellent positioning to me, and it kept my mind off the ITB pain as we ascended past encouraging costumed cheerleaders and taunting devils on the longest climb of the course: Old Sauk Pass. Two more steep climbs stood in our way before we steered into the excitement of Verona.

The town of Verona throws a huge party on Ironman Sunday, and between trips to the barbecue pit, people lined the town's main street to cheer riders in a Tour de France-like party atmosphere. Hundreds of screaming people, photographers and TV crews greeted us as we reached mile 56, halfway home. It should be an uplifting point in the race, and it was, briefly, for me. Unfortunately, I was rapidly feeling the first signs of an approaching bonk, signs that my race was beginning to fall apart way too early.

I had unintentionally not taken in enough Gatorade early on, and I was beginning to pay the price. Before the race, I decided to use only one bottle cage, to be more streamlined, assuming I'd reload at aid stations every 10 miles. The first aid station was 17 miles from the start, so I got behind because I had expected one earlier. Then I foolishly skipped taking a bottle at the 2nd and 4th aid stations because I hadn't completely finished the bottle I was carrying, and I was feeling good. I reasoned that I didn't want to be carrying extra weight, even in liquid form. Foolish rookie mistake by this veteran; saving a few ounces of weight was having too high a cost.

Shortly after Verona, the dehydration began to hit hard. I was feeling sore much earlier than usual and really getting thirsty. Staring at my empty Gatorade bottle, in a panic, I realized I had many miles to go to get to the next aid station, at mile 70 in Mt. Horeb. I tried to stay near Barry, but he slipped out of sight for good while I was fading and trying to control the damage. As the sun rose and the temperatures climbed into the 80s, I felt like I was drying up in the desert. Everything had been going perfectly. How could I have let this happen?

Sometimes I wish there was a flight data recorder to capture all the feelings, emotions and thoughts that occur during the Ironman bike ride, especially during the bad moments. The mind scrambles in a million directions as the body approaches Apollo 13 territory: there's been an explosion, now the question is — how to get back to earth in one piece from here? How do I not only survive the next few miles, but how can to put it back together to support the rest of the race? During some of these worst moments, I tried to find positive things to keep me going: images of friends made me smile; music constantly ran through my head, I was trying to absorb positive energy from the people, the action, and the sights and sounds around me. Dealing with these moments can be brutal, but they are also defining.

As I finally approached the next aid station in Mt. Horeb at mile 70, a rider passed me and asked how I was doing. I told him honestly: I'm bonking. He sneered back with words to the effect of 'you're not going to make it,' and sped by as if I was history. It made me mad, which was a good thing. It gave me the jolt I needed; I knew I'd prove him wrong, and noted his number. I was going to blow this guy off the course by the time the day was done. Just not at that minute; I needed to down 48 ounces of fluid, fast, and here was the aid station I had been hazily dreaming about for the last 30 minutes.

Aid station by aid station, I slowly pulled myself out of the deepest bonk I'd ever experienced on a bike course. I overcompensated — I took two 24 oz bottles at every station, and tried to force myself back to normal. I staggered through the rollers, the steep Old Sauk Road climb, and the two others, and it was coming back, but not fast enough. I normally take pain reliever and salt tablets at mile 100, but I gave in and took them at mile 90. Good move. All of a sudden, I started feeling better, and by the time I reached Verona for the second and last time, at mile 90, I was riding out of the saddle and thinking about making up time.

There's nothing like passing the mile 100 marker on an Ironman bike course, and feeling strong. After 40 miles dragging myself out of the hell of dehydration, there I was, heading back toward Madison, picking up speed again. The old me was back, passing rider after rider. The guy who sneered at me? I caught him at mile 105, and left him in my dust. Take that!

In the last miles on the bike course, I checked the readings on my bike computer, and they looked great. My speeds were coming back up, and it looked like I was going to have the ride of my life after all. All the long training rides, the speed of my new Softride Rocket, and the vision I had outlined before the race were coming together. As I had hoped before the race, I did in fact explode on the bike. It's just that I didn't intend it quite so literally, the good with the bad. Pulling up the four-story helix to enter the second transition, I had done what I set out to do: at 5:32:10, I had shaved several minutes off my 2002 Wisconsin bike split, and had delivered my fastest Ironman bike ride ever.

When done with the bike, back up the four story helix, change to running shoes, and out onto the two-loop 26.2 mile run course through the hilly state capitol and university areas. Because of the long transition zone, expect a 0:04:00 T2.

With the 112th fastest bike ride on the day, I had passed 466 riders, and when I handed my bike to a transition volunteer I was in 172nd place overall. Buoyed by this success, I sped through the second transition as fast as I could. I changed into the same Brooks Trance running shoes that had carried me to a 3:37 marathon at rain-soaked Ironman USA in Lake Placid a month earlier, put my Met-Rx hat on, and ran out the door having spent only 2:07 in transition.

Run

As happy as I was entering the run course for the first time ever with less than seven hours elapsed in an Ironman, I knew one thing: everything that had happened to this point suddenly didn't matter. It all comes down to how fast you can run the marathon. And I wanted to run a fast one.

I want to run my fastest Ironman marathon and that means I need to run faster than 3:33. I was too foggy to read the pace on my watch last year, but I need to pay close attention to times each mile. I need to average 8 minutes per mile to run a 3:30:xx. I think this will require pushing harder than I ever have before, so I hope I'm feeling decent when the time comes.

I had to admit I was feeling better than earlier in the day, but not as good as when I ran that 3:33 in Lake Placid 2002. Just shy of 2:00pm, I entered the run course with the temperature above 90 degrees, knowing that the next words I wrote before the race couldn't have been more on target:

"At this point in the race everything's up in the air, and it takes a perfect balance of previous effort, conservation, nutrition, hydration and conditions for a perfect run. All I can say is I will be going as hard as I can, and the clock will read whatever it reads at the end. The point of the journey is not to arrive; anything can happen."

I knew that I had not maintained that perfect balance and that a perfect run would, in fact, require pushing harder than ever before. This was going to be interesting.

The two-loop Ironman Wisconsin run course is unique in that it circulates through the center of Madison and its university, while other courses tend to mainly lie out of the main town. I had intended to run fast, and the first few miles went much better than the 8 minute pace I had wanted. My first mile, to and away from the Capitol was my fastest in an Ironman marathon: 6:41. Too fast. I eased back on the second, taking my first pit stop all day, and clocking a 7:56 on Spring Street, heading towards the football stadium. At this point, I finally caught up with Barry, who had entered the run course a couple minutes ahead of me. I passed him quickly but had the sense that he would hold on for a solid finish.

The next two miles to Observatory Drive were at 7:33 pace, and I began to wonder how fast this run might be. The combination of impending soreness and the steepest climb of the day led me to walk part of mile 5, and it came in at 9:24. But I got back on track with the next two miles, running 8:03 miles past wonderfully supportive spectators on State Street, and onto the shaded lakefront bike path.

But as soon as we approached blazing sun in an open field, the gears began grinding as hunger and dehydration became problems again. Mile 8 was an 8:22, and I knew I was slipping fast. At mile 9 on Walnut Street, both quads seized threateningly, and I knew if they didn't get better, I was in trouble again. Feeling like I was now running in quicksand, I began ignoring my watch, and focused on simply trying to save my run.

I had been carefully taking in at least a cup of Gatorade and a cup of Cola at aid stations every mile on the run, but it wasn't enough. There were probably also lingering effects from the bike bonk that were coming back to bite me. I began shuffling from aid station to aid station, downing a nausea-inducing combination — Gatorade, Cola, Water, GU gels, and where possible, chicken soup. At mile 11, I drank three cups of the soup to try to rebuild my sodium levels. The wheels were coming off my marathon, and I was hoping that something in that blend would help.

I moved on — I hesitate to call it running at that point because I don't think I was going very fast. But I did notice something important: no one had passed me, and I seemed to still be moving faster than others. I returned to the Capitol, registering a 1:50 half marathon time but I didn't even notice. I was just adhering to the last part of the pre-race plan: "I will be going as hard as I can, and the clock with read whatever it reads at the end."

As the intensity of the heat increased, and more people around me stopped running altogether, I remembered that in similar conditions at June's Ironman Idaho, 230 out of 1574 participants were unable to finish the course. Barry had raced there, too, and his 4 hour marathon was 100th fastest overall. So I had the feeling that even though I was going slower than hoped, it was due to conditions, and I had the very real chance of placing well in the marathon.

Miles 14 to 19 were a complete blur of tunnel vision to me, except for the wonderful spectators calling out support. There were apparently many xtri.com readers out there and I really appreciated the shouts of encouragement all day. They helped me come back to reality and I finally glanced at my watch again with 9:20 elapsed in the race, and about seven miles to go. For some reason, at that moment, a spark ignited the fuse. It was as if I had been given a new battery. I lit up inside, and said to myself: 'now or never, time to Lean Into It.'

The next seven miles were going to determine if I was going to earn a spot to Kona 2004 in this race. Last year at this same point, I had the distinct feeling, with no real reason, that I could get 10th in my age group. This year, I also had a distinct feeling, but it was about overall placing. I was feeling like 80th overall was possible, compared to 139th overall in 2002. I didn't really see that many people ahead, and no one had yet passed me. Well, one person did speed by me at mile 17, but ten minutes later he had passed out at the side of the road, and I never saw him again.

The final three miles of Ironman Wisconsin were slightly but painfully uphill, culminating in a short but steep climb to the Capitol. As I approached the last few hundred meters, I spotted and tried to pass what seemed like an endless number of runners. Unsure of who was on their first or second lap, as much as it hurt, I had to try to pass each one. Coming to the final right hand turn onto MLK Drive, and seeing the finish 100 meters away, I remembered Barry's 6-second near miss in Canada two weeks earlier, and couldn't take any chances. I broke into a full-on sprint for the finish, and charged over the line in 10:38:24.

I had no idea at the time, but I had just completed the breakthrough run of 2003 that I had been seeking. I had run the 57th fastest marathon overall, and had finished in 62nd place overall, by far my best Ironman finish ever. The best part: 6th place M40-44, and Kona 2004 Qualification. Icing on the cake: twenty-two minutes later, my training partner Barry Schliesmann crossed the line, and realized his Kona dream, too.

Kona 2003: Racing the Sunset

"Only those who have come to this place . . . and have done the work . . . know the feeling . . ."

For most of the previous year, these words, spoken by Al Trautwig during NBC's 2002 Ironman broadcast, ran repeatedly through my mind during hard training efforts and races. I had been a rookie at the 2002 Ironman Triathlon World Championship in Kona, and as a finisher, I knew the unique feeling. The words served to remind me what I was gunning for this year. Returning as a veteran age-grouper to the Ironman World Championship after a challenging and ultimately successful 2003 season, I felt I better understood the island and the course, and I was ready to race.

At 6am on race morning, walking toward bodymarking I ran into Marc Herremans, who was also ready to race. Herremans, a Belgian triathlete who finished 6th in Kona in 2001, had been poised to return with a shot to win in 2002. Instead, a tragic accident left him paralyzed from the waist-down, limiting his abilities, but not his resolve. His 2002 attempt to compete was inspiring to everyone who saw it, and even though he had to drop out, he vowed to return. I walked up to him and shook his hand. 'It's amazing that you are here.' I told him. 'You are outstanding, and an inspiration.' I hoped he would do well.

An hour later, I joined Marc and 1646 other triathletes in Kailua Bay for the start of the 25th Anniversary Ironman Triathlon World Championship. Looking at the sky while treading water, it was remarkable to see the moon that had been so awesome in the dark when I left the hotel at 4am was still high in the clear blue sky. A nice moment of calm before everything started.

Last year's Ironman swim was reportedly among the toughest on record. The water was so churned up, I saw nothing below the surface, and above, I saw whitecaps. I just tried to hang on, and I had finished in 1:18:57. Unsure of what to expect this time, before the race I said I'd love a calm swim, maybe in the 1:15:xx range.

In stark contrast to rain and choppy waves last year, this year the sun was out and the water was calm for the 7am start. I waited for the cannon, and then we were off. Immediately, I knew things were different from last year. Amid the typical chaos of the Ironman swim start, there was peace below as schools of fish continued their business, unfazed. The visibility was spectacular, like an aquarium. I've never enjoyed an Ironman swim as much.

Currents helped scoot me out to the halfway point in no time, and I temporarily entertained thoughts that I might actually be a decent swimmer. The pack of swimmers around me seemed so graceful and fluid, and I felt lucky to be among them. This feeling didn't last, unfortunately, as the chop and currents picked up, and I swallowed salt water several times on what seemed like a trip on a water treadmill back to shore. While I did shave some time from 2002, it was less than I expected, and I crossed the timing mat in 1:17:12.

The new transition area behind the King K hotel was great – spacious, well-organized, and easy to navigate. I had no trouble finding my bike-to-run transition bag, one reason being that 1168 people had exited the water before me, and most bags in my area were already long gone. I put on my cycling shoes, jersey and helmet, grabbed my bike, and set off to try to move a few hundred spots closer to the leaders.

Kona is renowned for its winds, and I knew my bike experience could be unpredictable depending on conditions. I'm told the winds were relatively calm last year, when I rode a 6:01:54 still having felt I battled strong headwinds on the way home. Before the race, I told friends I'd like to see a 5:50:xx bike split, but would do my best against what was out there.

Pedaling out of transition, I felt terrific, ready for a good ride. After spending the first 77 minutes of the race gazing at fish in the ocean, it was great to begin seeing people, starting with friends watching at the side of the road, then athletes I recognized on the course. Some were doing well, others not. Three miles into the ride I saw unhappy pro Wendy Ingraham sitting next to her bike, her race apparently over. On the other side of the road dozens of riders were speeding back from the first turnaround, including wheelchair athlete Randy Caddell, followed in hot pursuit by Marc Herremans. They were flying.

After 10 miles, I was on the Queen K with them and everyone else, riding north into the endlessness of the lava fields. The winds seemed similar to 2002, but I was riding faster. For the first 30 miles to Waikoloa, I averaged 21.8 mph, up from 20.4mph a year earlier. Things were starting better than in 2002. Maybe because I was more in tune with the course and the island. Like a veteran.

The next 30 miles including the long climb to mile 60 in Hawi also went reasonably well at 18.8 mph, compared to 17.9 mph the previous year. I was feeling stronger, attributing it to better long training rides during the year, and my upgrade to the Softride Rocket. An apparent tailwind didn't hurt, either. On my way up to Hawi, I noticed a dozen or so lead pro cyclists screaming back towards Kona on the other side in a pack that looked too comfortably tight to be true.

After I made the turn in Hawi, it turned out I was right about that tailwind. Headwinds on the downhill slowed me to 20.0 mph for the next 28 miles to Waikoloa, compared to a breezy 20.8 mph in 2002. But this time, I began to really appreciate the beauty of where I was. A day earlier, I had taken photos of the ocean views here, and had shared them with friends. When I reached these spots in the race, it was like living in the middle of those photos.

I was soon brought back to reality when I saw Marc Herremans coming from the opposite direction, powering his way in a handcycle uphill towards Hawi. He was followed shortly by Dick Hoyt pulling his son Ricky, a quadriplegic with cerebral palsy, up the hill on his bike. Inspiring to see, these are each incredible athletes.

In 2002, I had I reached mile 90 near Waikoloa averaging 20mph, feeling confident, foolishly thinking I might hold that pace. I was in for a rough surprise that veterans know well; the strong headwinds for the remainder of that ride had me panting at 13-15mph, and not feeling too happy. This year was different. At this point, I was still feeling strong, from the training, the bike, and possibly a new experiment — a salt tablet every 10 miles. It seemed to help. And that veteran experience – knowing what to expect – made a difference.

Soon, Larry Parker passed me on my right. The 2002 NBC Ironman coverage had featured Parker, an NYPD firefighter who was racing to commemorate the spirit of the 343 New York firefighters who lost their lives during 9/11. He was back, and again, sporting a jersey with the names of each lost fireman. I pulled up aside of him, shook his hand, then we rode on for the last 25 miles through headwinds back towards town averaging 17.7 mph. I finished the ride well ahead of expectations in 5:43:58, 17 minutes better than in 2002, having passed 516 athletes. Excellent.

Now, I was ready to run. I ran 3:50:14 in the heat last year, but I told friends I'd do better this time. Having run a 2:55:26 marathon in Milwaukee thirteen days earlier, I felt in solid marathon form. My target, in the 3:45:xx range, had me finishing the race in about 10:55:xx.

Reaching Alii Drive on the first miles heading south to the first turnaround, I saw friends at roadside who had been following me around the course all day. Each time I saw them it brought a smile and a burst of speed, and I reached the turnaround after running 5.3 miles averaging 7:37 per mile. This was a marked improvement compared to 2002, when I covered the same ground at 8:04/mile pace. It turned out that these fast first miles would make the main difference in my overall marathon time compared to 2002.

At mile 10, I caught up with Missy LeStrange, a 51 year-old legend who has won many age group titles in Hawaii. She had missed the 2002 race due to injury, and she wanted to reclaim her status as age group champion this year. As I reached her just before the Palani Drive incline out of town, she was receiving word from her spotter that she was in the lead of her age group by 25 minutes. She was doing incredibly well, and we headed out toward the Energy Lab, passing athletes along the way.

As I reached miles 13 and 14 on the run – halfway between town and the Energy Lab, it seemed that this was a point some breakdowns were occurring. It was near here that defending champ Tim DeBoom, closing within 300 yards of race leader Peter Reid, had earlier been forced by injury to drop out. In real time, two other elite athletes were reeling from dashed expectations. Chris McCormack, once among the lead men, was on the other side of the road, having been reduced to a walk back to town. And Ironman Idaho and Wisconsin champ Heather Gollnick's reported knee problems slowed her to the point that I overtook her, to my surprise. To McCormack's and Gollnick's credit, they both finished what they started, making it to the finish no matter how long it took.

Rounding the turn at mile 18 deep in the Energy Lab loop, Michael Fisch, a friendly rival, called out to me. As in Ironman USA Lake Placid earlier this year, he was stalking me from behind, and running well. I had covered the previous 12.4 miles at 8:52/mile pace and I was fading, though probably not unlike just about everyone else.

Michael shouted a private mantra we share, and it picked me up when I needed it.

I pulled out of the Energy Lab, took the right turn at about mile 19 onto the Queen K highway, and headed back toward town with a new sense of urgency, if not speed. Something interesting happened at this turn. It was as if everyone in front of me looked at their watch, said to themselves 'hey, I can finish under 11 hours', and began running collectively harder. One of these people was Julie Moss, and I caught up with her at about mile 22.

A 45 year-old Ironman hall-of-famer, Moss's complete collapse and gutsy finish in on ABC in 1982 put triathlon on the map for the first time. This finish will be forever depicted as one of the great moments in triathlon, and it's gripping. After having seen it often over the years, it was nice to be able share a few hundred yards and to thank her in person for what she had done for this sport. Then I moved on, racing the sunset to the finish.

Long before I ever entertained the idea of racing in Kona, I knew that for those who go, finishing before sundown is an ultimate goal. On this day, the sun was due to set at 5:58pm, with lingering daylight until 6:20pm. In 2002, I was close, but it was nearly dark when I finished at 6:17pm. This time, as I approached the final uphill at mile 24, I glanced over my right shoulder at the setting sun, I was increasingly certain I would beat it home. The race was on.

Rounding the corner at the Queen K Highway and Palani Drive at about the 25 mile point was special. In 2002, I had passed this point alone and quietly struggling, but this year I was feeling reasonably great, picking up speed toward the finish. My friends were waiting at the next turn by a big sign that said 'One Mile to Go', and by then I felt like I had wings.

After being near racers all day, it seemed like I had the final 200 yards to the finish on Alii Drive — the best final stretch in this sport — all to myself. Wrapping up a 3:46:58 marathon, and after passing 173 runners, the clock ahead read 10:55:27. It was 5:55pm, and the sun had not yet set. I had come to this place, I had done the work, and I knew the feeling. I don't think I've ever smiled so broadly for a finish before.

Over the next few minutes, other sunset-racers who had shared parts of the day with me arrived for their own Ironman finish, including Julie Moss, Missy LeStrange, Michael Fisch and Larry Parker. As daylight passed, I heard that Marc Herremans was on the run course. Incredibly, he made good on the commitment he had made one year ago, crossing the line again, this time in a wheelchair, in 13:24:25. Outstanding.

Breaking Barriers

- Qualifying Training Plan Strategy Year 3
- Kona Slot #4: Ironman USA Lake Placid 2004
- Kona 2004: In Memory of . . .

Qualifying Training Plan Strategy Year 3

The year 2004 was what I'd consider my third year as a reasonably competitive age group triathlete. Before 2002, I had competed well, surviving and finishing with generally respectable times in most races, but I had not taken my performance to the next level.

In 2002, I got to that next level, setting several personal bests on the way to my first qualification for Ironman Hawaii in Kona. In reviewing that year, I wrote that the key to my improvement was threefold: upping my average training time per week to about 8.5 hours, training harder and racing earlier in the season, and a significant shift to more emphasis on cycling. By year's end, I had spent 44% of my training time cycling (38% run, 18% swim), and the results showed.

The 2003 season was strong, but not as good, taking several months to build to what I believed to be a satisfactory performance level. I had fretted early in the year, feeling like my results were lagging, and my training log showed my training fell short of 2002 levels. For 2003, I averaged a full hour less training, 7.5 hours per week. I started the year 2003 slowly, not training as intensely as in 2002. I tried to adhere to the same mix of training time as in 2002, and for the most part achieved it: 46% bike, 43% run, 11% run. That one-hour less training time translated to about 40 minutes less swimming and 20 minutes less cycling. Not awful, and I finally returned to form late in the year, qualifying for the Kona 2004 race in Wisconsin.

So how did 2004 go? A mixed bag that I'd consider a success, but with unmistakable trouble spots. Overall, I split the difference between 2002 and 2003, averaging a little more than 8 hours of training per week. I knocked 21 minutes off my Ironman PR at Ironman USA Lake Placid in July, for a 10:12:22 that would have earned a 2005 Kona slot, had I needed it. I won the masters division at Mad-City Marathon in May, going 2:58:12 in pouring rain, and I was proud of that.

But 2004 also had some of my worst performances in years, and disappointments I never expected. My season-opening half marathon was an atrociously slow 1:29:37, several minutes slower than I'd run in years at that distance. A month later, similar story with a 3:09:06 in the heat at the Boston Marathon. In August, I struggled in the water at the Olympic Distance Chicago Triathlon, and two weeks later, I nearly DNFd on the run at Ironman Wisconsin. I also did not qualify for Kona 2005 in Wisconsin, failing on one of my annual goals.

2002 to 2004 Training Summary Comparison

Swim, Bike, Run

	2002	2003	2004
Miles	5,324.8	5,033.5	5,187.0
Time	443:09:45	392:25:00	422:35:46
Sessions	390	351	392
Distance/Session	13.65	14.34	13.23
Time/session	1:08:11	1:07:05	1:04:41
Time/mile	04:59.6	04:40.7	04:53.3
Time/week	8:31:20	7:32:47	8:06:16

Swim

	2002	2003	2004
Miles	146.3	83.7	101.6
Time	78:27:19	44:19:34	53:00:26
Sessions	121	81	88
Distance/Session	1.21	1.03	1.16
Time/session	0:38:54	0:32:50	0:36:08
Time/mile	32:10.2	31:47.4	31:17.4

Bike

	2002	2003	2004
Miles	3,830.8	3,577.8	3,452.7
Time	196:47:00	179:58:59	168:43:20
Sessions	129	131	127
Distance/Session	29.70	27.31	27.19
Time/session	1:31:32	1:22:26	1:19:43
Time/mile	03:04.9	03:01.1	02:55.9

Run

	2002	2003	2004
Miles	1,347.7	1,372.0	1,632.7
Time	167:55:26	168:06:27	200:52:00
Sessions	140	139	177
Distance/Session	9.63	9.87	9.22
Time/session	1:11:58	1:12:34	1:08:05
Time/mile	07:28.6	07:21.1	07:22.9

2004 By The Numbers

So, let's take a look into a mixed training and racing year, and try to pull out the lessons from what worked and what didn't. First, let's review the numbers for 2004:

1. Swim: 88 swim sessions, 101 miles, 53 hours total; average swim 1.2 miles; total 1.9 miles per week
2. Bike: 127 bike rides, 3,452 miles, 168 hours; average ride 27 miles; total 66 miles per week
3. Run: 177 runs, 1,632 miles, 201 hours; average run 9.2 miles; total 31 miles per week
4. Total: 392 workouts, 5,187 miles, 422 hours; average 8 hours 6 minutes per week
5. Longest workout week: 18 hours – 13 bike, 3 run, 2 swim; three weeks before Ironman USA Lake Placid in July
6. Number of training weeks over 10 hours: 12; six of those included Ironman, 50k or marathon races

It's worth pointing out that annual averages can be a little misleading, especially training time. While the year averaged a little over 8 hours training/racing per week, the effort really broke down into three stages:

*   Weeks 1 to 13: averaging 6 hours 21 minutes per week, mostly running
*   Weeks 14 to 42: heavy racing season, averaging 10 hours 58 minutes per week
*   Weeks 43 to end of year: post-season cool-down, 5 hours 45 minutes per week

Next, let's look behind the numbers.

2004 Training Summary: Time, Miles and Races

2004 Totals

Data	Bike	Run	Swim	Grand Total
Sum of Distance	3,452.69	1,632.70	101.64	5,187.03
Sum of Time	168:43:20	200:52:00	53:00:26	422:35:46
Count of Type	127	177	88	392
Avg Dist/Exercise	27.19	9.22	1.16	13.23
Avg Time/Exercise	1:19:43	1:08:05	0:36:08	1:04:41
Avg Time/mile	02:55.9	07:22.9	31:17.4	04:53.3
Time/day	0:27:44	0:33:01	0:08:43	1:09:28
Time/week	3:14:09	3:51:08	1:01:00	8:06:16
Dist/week	66.22	31.31	1.95	99.48

Major Races	Date	Time
Chicago 50k Ultramarathon	April	4:02:03
Boston Marathon	April	3:09:06
MadCity Marathon	May	2:58:12
North Shore Half Marathon	June	1:22:46
Ironman USA Lake Placid	July	10:12:22
Chicago Triathlon	August	2:18:59
Ironman Wisconsin	September	10:52:30
Ironman World Champsionship	October	11:51:08

Swim

I know, still too little time swimming in 2004. Not much different than previous years. A few things work against me, beginning with swimming being a third priority for me. I know my swim competency has improved in recent years, but the work required to find a few extra minutes on race day translates to more hours than I have. Life gets in the way, between work, four kids that keep getting older and more involved with things that require my time (which I happily give). And I still don't like to swim all that much, honestly.

The way my life works, with the limited time I have to train in the first place, I try to get the most out of those hours, and in recent years, that's meant more time on the bike, at the sacrifice of less time in the water.

What was the result of less attention to swimming in 2004? Just about a 2 minute increase on my best Ironman swim, to 1:09 at Ironman USA Lake Placid. Not bad, not preferable. Still needs to improve.

Run

Before we talk about the bike, those who paid close attention to the numbers will say: wait a minute Ray, you talk about the importance of more time on the bike . . . then why did your run workouts clearly outnumber you bike sessions?

It all goes back to my early season struggles, the roughest I'd encountered in years. I didn't feel my training was going well in late winter, but I didn't panic at first. But when I struggled in the half marathon in March, my worst fears seemed confirmed. I didn't have it anymore, I thought. Nothing seemed to be clicking, whether it was swimming, biking or running.

My confidence was falling fast, and I decided to just try to restore it one discipline at a time. From the middle of March to the end of May (Mad-City Marathon), eight weeks, basically all I did was run. I needed to find the speed and comfort in something, and running was it. If I rode the bike or swam, they were mainly recovery cross-training efforts.

2004 Training Summary: Weekly Hours

Weekly Time

Sum of Time	Type			
Week	Bike	Run	Swim	Grand Total
1	1:57:01	2:32:09		4:29:10
2	1:58:17	2:59:52		4:58:09
3	2:00:16	3:00:33	0:24:36	5:25:25
4	1:58:59	1:28:01		3:27:00
5	3:57:23	2:22:34		6:19:57
6	2:30:40	3:18:02	1:01:30	6:50:12
7	2:25:48	3:06:59	0:30:04	6:02:51
8	2:30:55	2:45:40	1:32:37	6:49:12
9	1:58:58	2:58:04		4:57:02
10	2:20:00	3:29:15	1:01:47	6:51:02
11	0:56:45	3:51:08	1:53:23	6:41:16
12	2:13:54	2:00:00	1:02:26	5:16:20
13	0:29:43	2:51:24		3:21:07
14		8:39:03	1:36:00	10:15:03
15	0:30:00	3:16:30	0:44:27	4:30:57
16	0:45:00	3:42:16	0:45:20	5:12:36
17	1:01:29	5:20:36	0:20:06	6:42:11
18	1:32:17	5:50:47	2:25:36	9:48:40
19	0:30:08	7:13:15	1:47:42	9:31:05
20	0:59:30	7:00:20	1:21:45	9:21:35
21		7:30:55	0:30:21	8:01:16
22		3:25:00	1:25:27	4:50:27
23	4:43:13	5:12:56	1:24:17	11:20:26
24	5:55:57	1:53:57	0:32:52	8:22:46
25	4:08:50	5:05:03	1:01:12	10:15:05
26	8:40:27	2:48:06	1:34:37	13:03:10
27	10:01:24	3:12:56	1:19:25	14:33:45
28	12:47:15	3:39:44	2:01:30	18:28:29
29	6:27:11	3:41:32	1:36:16	11:44:59
30	4:42:34	2:10:07	1:07:39	8:00:20
31	11:11:00	6:05:05	1:43:49	18:59:54
32	7:38:08	2:40:01	2:08:40	12:26:49
33	4:10:39	3:15:58	1:54:50	9:21:27
34		4:08:20	3:54:57	8:03:17
35	8:49:11	2:36:29	2:33:55	13:59:35
36	4:51:32	2:59:37	1:01:03	8:52:12
37	2:09:23	3:37:30		5:46:53
38	7:15:51	5:44:57	1:41:22	14:42:10
39	3:44:12	3:24:36	1:33:20	8:42:08
40	0:59:22	0:38:40	0:39:43	2:17:45
41	1:10:31	4:08:53	1:02:26	6:21:50
42	6:15:00	6:36:57	1:18:47	14:10:44
43		1:48:11	0:52:39	2:40:50
44		3:48:32		3:48:32
45	0:30:04	2:42:57	0:35:22	3:48:23
46	1:17:58	1:38:13		2:56:11
47	0:37:15	5:47:05		6:24:20
48	0:30:00	7:34:39	0:25:37	8:30:16
49	2:10:33	2:46:26	1:01:09	5:58:08
50	3:07:30	6:20:38	0:29:40	9:57:48
51	5:00:20	1:12:48	1:02:12	7:15:20
52	3:16:52	1:45:58		5:02:50
53	3:54:05	3:02:46		6:56:51
Grand Total	168:43:20	200:52:00	53:00:26	422:35:46

The good news is, that strategy paid off. I regained the running form I wanted, with a 2:58:12 marathon in late May. I felt like I was back, and ready to launch into triathlon mode.

Another thing bloated my running numbers in 2004: the use of running as a way to cope with losses. After my grandmother died in May, and after my father died in October, I retreated to runs as a way to get out there, to keep going, to get through it. After Kona, I continued running as therapy through November, not really riding my bike at all, but continuing to run several times a week, just to think, to breathe, to survive.

Bike

Back to the shining part of the year – cycling. I had a best-ever year on the bike, despite putting in fewer miles than in 2002 or 2003. I won't say that the fewer hours helped. In fact I think more hours on the bike would have helped me get even better, but I was still pretty pleased as it was.

I rode 60 hours and 1180 miles indoors on CompuTrainer with PowerCranks, mainly from January to March, and in December. The average time for indoor rides was about 48 minutes and 16 miles. The rides were of shorter duration because indoor training mainly focused on drills, intervals, and getting stronger on the PowerCranks. Rarely did I ride more than one hour indoors in 2004, and that's something that's already changed in 2005.

The breakthroughs clearly came during my outdoor rides. When things got warm enough in Chicago, I rode 2,272 miles outside on my Softride Rocket in 109 hours. The average outdoor ride was 42 miles in 2 hours, the longest, furthest and fastest I've averaged in any year. As I wrote in an earlier xtri column, when I began serious bike training, I threw myself into it in search of faster speeds than ever. Early morning bike workouts became mini-time trials, and I'd try to wedge as many miles between 5am and the time I needed to drive my kids to school in the morning before heading to work. Each extra mile meant more speed. It was fun.

2004 Training Summary: Weekly Distance

Weekly Distance

Sum of Distance	Type			
Week	Bike	Run	Swim	Grand Total
1	33.9	20.3		54.1
2	40.0	20.4		60.4
3	38.2	23.2	0.8	62.1
4	40.0	11.0		51.0
5	79.3	16.6		95.9
6	50.0	25.4	1.8	77.2
7	50.0	24.4	0.9	75.3
8	50.0	22.1	2.8	74.9
9	39.1	23.2		62.3
10	44.8	26.8	1.9	73.6
11	19.0	29.8	3.6	52.3
12	41.8	15.8	2.0	59.6
13	10.0	24.3		34.3
14		67.8	2.9	70.7
15	9.7	28.5	1.4	39.6
16	15.0	32.2	1.4	48.6
17	20.0	43.6	0.6	64.2
18	30.0	49.4	4.6	84.0
19	9.0	61.1	3.4	73.5
20	20.0	60.9	2.6	83.4
21		63.9	1.0	64.9
22		29.5	2.7	32.2
23	91.0	43.9	2.7	137.6
24	122.5	17.0	1.1	140.6
25	88.2	42.9	2.0	133.0
26	181.8	23.3	3.1	208.2
27	211.0	27.8	2.6	241.4
28	270.7	30.4	3.9	305.0
29	140.0	30.6	3.1	173.7
30	104.5	18.9	2.2	125.5
31	233.6	48.0	3.4	285.0
32	161.9	23.3	4.0	189.2
33	91.9	28.6	3.9	124.4
34		34.2	7.2	41.4
35	187.7	22.7	5.0	215.4
36	107.3	25.4	2.0	134.7
37	47.5	30.6		78.1
38	148.8	38.8	3.4	191.0
39	71.9	30.1	3.1	105.1
40	20.3	6.2	1.3	27.8
41	21.0	32.9	2.1	56.0
42	112.0	45.9	2.4	160.3
43		14.8	1.7	16.5
44		31.8		31.8
45	10.0	22.0	1.2	33.2
46	25.0	13.3		38.3
47	10.0	45.2		55.2
48	10.0	60.2	0.9	71.1
49	39.9	21.7	2.0	63.6
50	59.6	52.1	1.0	112.7
51	101.0	10.0	2.0	113.0
52	65.9	14.8		80.7
53	78.0	25.5		103.5
Grand Total	3,452.7	1,632.7	101.6	5,187.0

Further, I mixed it up with more early morning mid-week bike/run brick training sessions. In June and July, when the sun was up earliest, I'd ride 40 miles and do a fast 10k, or ride 25 and run a fast 9 miles. It got me conditioned to run well off the bike.

The intense biking paid off with a 5:25 bike PR at Ironman USA Lake Placid, followed by a marathon PR same day, of 3:26. If there's one thing I will keep in place for 2005, it's my approach to outdoor cycling.

Health

There's one more angle that affected my season. Unexpected struggles in four major races may all be tied to breathing challenges that I've mentioned from time to time in my columns. I've been treating asthma for years, but never considered the possible impact of allergies. It was only in October when I skipped a favorite marathon because I was having so much trouble breathing, that I may have found an answer. I saw a specialist, and it turned out I had significant allergies to more than a few things that we all encounter outdoors, any of which could have been compromising breathing effectiveness. I'm now getting treated for allergies, and seem to be breathing better. I hope it holds through this year.

The reason I mention this is that the lesson for triathletes may be to pursue answers when things don't feel quite right. We tend to be so fit, so healthy, so in touch with our bodies, our strengths, our endurance, that when we struggle, we're perhaps not so quick to consider that something physical beyond our control may be affecting us. If things don't feel right, training more may not solve everything. Don't be afraid to get a second opinion.

Finding the Time

Often, I wonder how much better an athlete I might be if I trained more. But it's a question that will probably never get an answer. With four growing children and an active career as a telecom/technology executive, I continually remain constrained in terms of time available to train. I will never have the kind of life that encourages a couple of

2004 Training Summary: Weekly Hours Chart

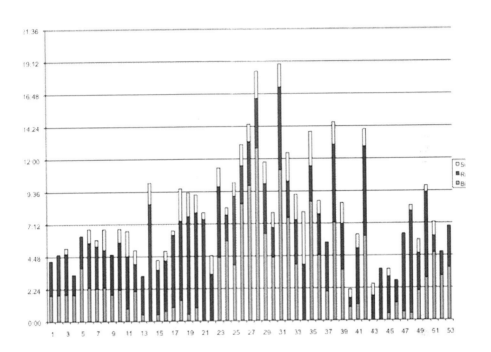

hours for training when I get home from work. I'd never consider it; there's the family to see, homework to help with, etc.

So when do I train? It's one of the most common questions I get. Simple answer: mainly when everyone else is asleep, at least during the week. In summer, as soon as there's daylight, I'm outside, and I'll train as long as I can before I drive kids to school and head to work. In winter, I train late at night indoors riding CompuTrainer or on the treadmill. On weekends, the longer the training effort, the earlier in the morning I will start, in an effort to be done by 10am at the latest. Soccer games to see, dance classes to take kids to, etc.

You dedicate the time you can to the things that matter. Keep priorities in order, enjoy what you do, enjoy the moment, live with spirit and strength. That's what 2004 was about

.

Kona Slot #4: Ironman USA Lake Placid 2004

Two weeks before the 2004 Ironman USA in Lake Placid, NY, I was on the other side of the country, watching the US Olympic Track and Field Trials in Sacramento California. On an evening where world class athletes were making the impossible look easy in a variety of running events, what stood out most was the high jump competition. The bar kept rising well beyond the height of the jumpers, ridiculously high. Yet the jumpers routinely defied the law of gravity, launching themselves to new levels.

It got me thinking about how high I've been able to raise the bar in my own racing since 1994. On reflection, I realized that in the last 10 years there were at least three different stages in my racing career where I was convinced I probably could raise the bar no further, and as of summer 2004, I was again stuck.

Marathon Plateau Ranges:
- 1995 to 1999 — 3:10 to 3:14
- 2000 to 2001 — 3:04 to 3:06
- 2002 to present 2:54 to 2:59

Ironman Plateau Ranges:
- 1997 to 2000 – 11 to 12 hours (and in May 2000, 13 hours. Ouch)
- 2000 to 2001 — Low 11-hours
- 2001 to July 2004– 10:33 to 10:50

At each plateau, I really had the feeling that maybe it couldn't get any better. Or maybe that it would require too much of a commitment, or radical change, to improve. And after the 2002 season, though I didn't want to admit it, that feeling kept creeping back. In each of the last two years, I've been asking myself: am I as good as I will ever be? is it possible to get better? If so, how? These questions are usually followed by: I'm getting older, with less available time; is it possible I might be on my way to getting worse?

For perspective, my personal best Ironman was achieved in Lake Placid in 2002: 10:33, with a 1:10 swim, 5:40 bike on the hilly course, 3:33 marathon (my best ever in an Ironman). I was at the top of my game that year, what I considered my best shape ever, I had finished 13th in the M40-44 age group on a tough course. While I've done well enough to qualify for Kona two times since then with several sub-11 hour finishes, I hadn't come within 5 minutes of that PR. Also, after a horrible start to the 2004 season, I was really concerned that my best racing was behind me.

Recent weeks have delivered definitive answers to those questions and concerns. Specifically, I lowered my Ironman PR by 21 minutes to 10:12:22 at Ironman USA Lake Placid with bike and marathon PRs in July, and set 1500 meter swim and 10k run PRs on my way to my first 'podium' at a local Olympic Distance triathlon two weeks later.

The main question people have been asking after raising the bar in recent weeks: what did you do differently?

1. Training Time (more? are you kidding?)

The thing I did not do was spend more time training. Not that it's a choice. As I get older, my kids get older, the job gets more demanding, there's less time in the day.

When I reviewed my 2002 training log in an xtri column, one of the things I concluded was the basis of that strong racing year was an increase in training time and miles. I had increased my average training time in the first 30 weeks of 2002 prior to Ironman USA to about 9.5 hours per week. By contrast, over the same period in 2004, I averaged less than 8 hours per week. Yes, both years had begun with low volume weeks, and had exceeded the weekly averages before race day, but still, there was a clear difference.

Avg Hours/Week preceding Ironman USA Lake Placid (Bike, Run, Swim, Total)

- 2002: 4:14:28, 3:26:01, 1:52:08, 9:32:37
- 2003: 3:21:15, 3:21:31, 0:46:22, 7:29:08
- 2004: 3:00:08, 3:52:53, 0:58:02, 7:51:03

So you couldn't say more training time was behind the improvements. But was it better training time?

2. Higher Quality Training

I don't even need to say it. With fewer hours, you need to get more out of them through higher quality training. But it's easier said than done. What does higher quality mean? For me this year, it meant raising the bar higher, and demanding to achieve higher speeds, regardless of time limits, particularly on the bike.

Just as I had racing plateaus, I also have had training plateaus. I remember in the late 1990s when averaging 20 mph on a single bike training ride was a huge deal. I remember later telling myself that 20mph must be the minimum, and it took a long time to get there. This year, I wanted to be comfortable averaging 21mph on training rides from 20 to 100 miles. That's a 5% improvement, and remembering what an effort it was to even get to that 20mph level, it seemed a real stretch.

But that goal became the focus, and to get there I had to try to find any advantage possible, with better form, higher cadence, or more strength pushing bigger gears. I forced myself to not be intimidated by seeing 25 mph on the bike computer, for example. You know how you can tell yourself: that's too fast! Try this: get to an impossible speed, then block out those negative thoughts; tell yourself YOU CAN. Then try to spend more time at that speed. What seemed beyond reach can soon seem normal, and you don't need a million training hours to get there.

3. Attitude

Even limitless training time and an abundance of hammer training sessions do not guarantee you good performance on race day. I know people who claim to train 20 to 25 hours per week who fizzle the second they pin their bib number on. I have trained with people who can endlessly crush me in workouts but cannot seem to get it together to have a good race. Putting in the time and effort may be enough to finish, but it's not enough to guarantee you the result you want or deserve.

The missing ingredient is Attitude. You need to head onto the race course knowing what you want to do, with the determination to do it, and the will to succeed even when the bar is seemingly beyond reach. I think back to those high jumpers at the Olympic Trials, each facing a bar that is physically higher than they are. Anyone would say it's impossible to get over something taller than yourself; these athletes say: let me at it! And they fly over it.

Putting it All Together

I did not have that will to succeed as the season opened. In a half marathon that I eventually finished with a time that I wouldn't even consider good for a training run, I had absolutely the wrong attitude. I ran defensively, hoping it wouldn't fall apart, and of course it did. My attitude, not my conditioning, had let it happen.

By July, I had the opposite approach. I went to Lake Placid buoyed by the new speeds I was seeing in my bike training, and with a May marathon finish under my belt that I knew few on the course could touch. The night before the race, I just had this feeling: I could not wait to get on the bike and run course and see how fast I could go. On the bike course, I was flying faster than ever before (eventually a 15 minute Lake Placid PR), and not concerned that I was pushing too hard. Determined to PR on the run, even at mile 8 I was saying to myself not the usual 'I hope I can hold on,' but 'I've never felt better at this point.' Confidence from training and the right attitude on the course can make the difference.

I was racing blind in Lake Placid – my watch had been kicked off during the swim, and my bike computer didn't work. I just went on feel. It was only when I saw the clock at about mile 24 did I know that I would PR by possibly 20 minutes or more. That was a significant movement of the bar. If you had asked me to consider it before the race, I would have said that was well over my head.

The top three US women high jump finishers that night in Sacramento all successfully sailed over 6 feet, 4.75 inches (1.95 meters). Impossible. But nobody told them, and now they will compete in Athens. Their lesson: don't limit yourself, and you can achieve your own impossible thing.

Looking back on my racing over the last 10 years, I see that too many times I stalled, thinking I might never get better. And, honestly, I will probably think the same thing again someday. But I need to keep in mind, and you should too: history can repeat, the bar can be raised, get your training and attitude right, and you can sail over that bar again and again.

Kona 2004: In Memory of . . .

It can take years to earn your trip to the Ironman Triathlon World Championship in Kona, Hawaii. And once you get there, you realize why the race, the course, and everything about the Ironman in Kona seems sacred. It's an amazing place, an amazing event, an amazing experience, no matter who you are, how you got there, and what you have to deal with out on the magical course. Even the unexpected.

Less than two weeks before the 2004 Ironman, my Dad, who was at my official Ironman debut in Canada in 1997, had stopped by our house to see my family and to ask about Kona preparations. Since that debut at Ironman Canada, he had traveled to see me race in Roth, Germany, Zurich Switzerland, and on return trips to Canada, always at similar places on the course, cheering and providing support. From those early, slower days, he knew how far I'd come to qualify and race in Hawaii.

He had also been with me at Kona 2002, from walking in the rain to the swim start, throughout the day, all the way to the end and beyond. On this visit before the 2004 race, he mentioned he was tempted to get a plane ticket and join me again. We smiled at the thought. He hugged my kids and he hugged me goodbye.

Two days later, Dad died suddenly and unexpectedly at 67 years old.

Our family waded numbly through the next few days, through the visitation and through the funeral, without an eye toward the calendar or other things happening in the world. Then my mother said to me, 'you're still going to Kona, right? He'd have wanted you to go. When is it again?"

Keep Going

The cannon was due to fire in Kailua Kona Bay less than six days after my father's funeral. I knew I had to go. He had been there in 2002, I sensed he would be there again this time. I've always said you can live a small lifetime on the racecourse in an endurance event. This time I knew I'd get that and more. I expected a small firestorm of memories and emotions on the course in Kona, and as tough as I knew that would be, I welcomed the thought of them. There is no better way to be alive than to feel deeply, I told myself.

As my Wednesday departure approached, I had no interest in getting ready. My bike and race gear were not packed until 30 minutes before leaving for the airport. On the plane headed to Kona I realized that I was physically ready to race, but mentally a million miles away. I hoped that would change once the plane touched down in Hawaii. Despite the company of great friends, and being in a magical place, it didn't.

The night before the race, emails arrived wishing good luck. In one reply, I just said it like it was:

"I'm trying to find a way to lighten this invisible load, and it's a little tough. Reminders of Dad here with me in 2002 are everywhere, from friends, to places to things.

"To have a great Ironman race here takes more than ability to get to the finish. You need an attitude that says 'attack', one that devours the course, and finds exceptional life in the process. It is simply indescribable when it works.

"However, honestly, I feel deflated at this moment, far from attack mode. That's dangerous; enter this course not on offense, it can eat you alive. I'm trying to find all the inspiring reasons to reverse this heavy feeling, and struggling."

Magic and Community at Ironman Hawaii

There is no Ironman swim more beautiful than the one in Kona, with great visibility, surrounded by talented swimmers. The bike course through the lava fields with legendary winds continues to be awe-inspiring, even if the winds added huge amounts of time to almost all racers. And there's nothing like making the turn to and from the

Energy Lab on the marathon course, and of course, the incomparable final steps on Alii Drive. You realize that every stroke you swim, every mile you ride, every step you run on the Ironman course in Kona is magical, special, regardless of your circumstances.

Undoubtedly there were people on the course this year carrying heavier loads than me. The inspiring physically challenged racers were unbelievable. There were certainly others who had lost loved ones and were also hoping to encounter them somewhere on the course. I was lucky to be racing healthy, while knowing that cancer survivors and even cancer sufferers, among others tackling health challenges, were making their way to the same finish as me.

As much as I was dealing with my own world that had changed, I was blessed and honored to be sharing the course with the entire community of Ironman athletes, volunteers, and supporters. I was alone with my thoughts all day on the course, and they were plentiful, but I also felt embraced by everyone and everything on the island. They helped me continue to go forward.

You can live a small lifetime on a race course, and it's over in the blink of an eye. That's exactly what happened to me in Kona 2004. The best summary of my race is contained in a blend of email excerpts composed just hours after the race, and they are below. They were my direct impressions of what amounted to a unique spiritual and personal adventure, and they tell the story, short as it was.

2004 Kona Race Notes

Once on the course, I realized how completely exhausted I was. I had totally underestimated what the previous days had taken from me, and was a shell of myself. That's a tough thing to realize with hours and hours to go, in a place that unforgiving. But I wasn't there for me; I was there for Dad. Trying to celebrate life, even if it hurt. A lot.

The winds in Kona this year were powerful and unrelenting almost from the start. I've been frustrated and have even cursed less formidable wind on Ironman bike courses in six different countries. This time as the winds kept coming, a lyric from a song I like immediately popped to mind: '. . . in the wind, he's still alive . . .' and ran through my head over and over. It made sense.

With this thought, I never complained internally. Instead I tried to figure out what Dad and others might be doing with this wind. Trying to make the experience more legendary? At 6:15 it was my longest time on a bike in 4 years (most felt the same way about their times), but I never felt insistent that it should end. I felt I was supposed to be there, feeling that wind.

But I was so exhausted. I started the run even with the thought of just walking. I made it running to five miles then had to shut down. I had nothing left in me, and everything of the last two weeks came crashing on my shoulders. I did stop and walk then, and decided that I would only run when I could, would walk if I needed, and would just finish. Given that, I did not run badly. I chatted with a few people I was near, talked about Dad, and that felt good.

The last miles were in pitch dark. A good opportunity to have a short conversation with Dad, to thank him, to say I missed him, and finally to say: 'let's go, time to finish.'

As I approached the line, announcer Mike Reilly had picked up word from a friend and called out my name, saying I was running for my Dad who passed away two weeks ago. I did not break down there; there had been plenty of that on the course.

It was very hard, very powerful, very right, very magical. I can't believe I did it.

Principles and Lessons from the Road to Kona

- Structure: Planning Your Season
- Efficiency: How Much Training Time?
- Balance: Tracking Your Training
- Execution: Everything Else You Need to Know

Structure: Planning Your Season

Some of you are ready to make a hard run at qualifying for Kona this year. Others may be preparing for their first Ironman with Kona a distant goal.

Whatever your starting point, the following applies to you: What do you want to achieve in your racing season?

Set Your Goals

Your goals can obviously cover a wide range, from participating in a race for the first time, to trying a new endurance sport, to competing in a new/different/longer/faster race, to setting new personal bests, to simply having fun. Take your pick, all potential goals have great merits.

I can honestly say that in my career of training for endurance events, I have had each of the above goals at one time or another. Some examples of my goals in different years:

- 1994: Finish a marathon.
- 1995: Knock 90 minutes off my marathon time to qualify for Boston
- 1997: Complete an Ironman triathlon.
- 2001: Run a sub-3 hour marathon.
- 2002: Qualify for the Kona
- 2004: Set an Ironman triathlon Personal Best.
- 2006: Enjoy training and racing for fun again.
- 2007: Racing with a new perspective, photographing ultramarathons, Ironmans, and marathons while racing in them.
- 2008: honestly, just to finish the Boston Marathon, and cover the Chicago Marathon as a journalist

Whatever your goal, I applaud it. Good for you. Now, let's set some parameters to help you get there.

Pick Your Race(s)

Nothing helps focus the pursuit of athletic goals like a target date or event. Races, with a clear deadline staring at you from your calendar, can be the motivating factor that helps guide your training.

Further, you probably have so sign up for your chosen event(s) pretty soon, even though the season may be months away. Popular races, including the Chicago Marathon and Chicago Triathlon, are reaching capacity limits earlier each year, and thousands of hopefuls are shut out of registration. Have to act fast these days.

You may also want to consider scheduling other races before the Big Event(s), just for practice. For me – but not necessarily for others – competing in a race per month during the season has many benefits, including gauging your fitness at that point and providing practice during race conditions but in an event that means less to you.

For example, when my goal was to complete an Ironman, it was a daunting challenge. I had never done anything that was remotely as difficult or time-consuming. That was part of the appeal of the goal, but it also had me worried about preparation.

So what I did was schedule a series of race events that would help build endurance and experience at longer races month after month, as well as sharpening speed later in the season.

As a guide of how I approached that Ironman debut season, here is the partial race schedule I followed.

- **April**: Boston Marathon: rarely a fast race, coming so early in the year; just a first long endurance effort
- **April**: Lake County Marathon (since discontinued): a week after Boston, this second marathon (you could insert a long run) simulated the challenge of an endurance effort without recovery time
- **May**: Ice Age Trail 50 mile race, in Wisconsin. Not that I was really inspired to run 50 miles, but I wanted to find out what it was like to remain in continuous motion longer than I had ever tried, with aid stations along the way.
- **June**: North Shore ½ Marathon, Highland Park, IL. After a series of endurance efforts, this race was a great one for what I call speed training. A high intensity workout but less time on your feet, still practicing race conditions.
- **July**: Find a favorite 4th of July 5k race and hammer it. But ride your bike for an hour first. Make this run the end of a speed brick, where you give it all you can on the bike and on the run. You are fine tuning for your triathlon.
- **August**: Chicago Triathlon. Moving from a speed brick race scenario in July, I used the Chicago Triathlon Olympic Distance

event as full-on swim, bike and run speed training, just two weeks before my first Ironman triathlon. It gave me the confidence to know I was ready

- **August:** Ironman Canada: with several positive events behind me – long endurance efforts and shorter faster ones, I stepped on an Ironman course that had intimidated me greatly months earlier, and turned my goal into a reality.

A couple of notes on the above schedule. First, it's probably not something you should worry about mirroring if you have a schedule that allows reasonable training time. During that year, including time in races, I averaged less than 6 hours training per week, so I had to lean on race experience to make up for limited training. What you might be able to invest in terms of time in long training days, I effectively turned into race days.

Second, of course, adjust the types of events, and frequency, according to your goal. If your big event is a 10k earlier in the year, adjust relative to your timing, with the main point remaining the same: build up to your goal with appropriate training and/or events.

Map Your Plan

Whether you're pursuing two races or twelve, having your season outlined gives you the structure to take the next step: mapping the training plan to meet your goal.

Creating a training plan seems deceptively simple. Millions of hopeful athletes do it every January. Take a spreadsheet, create a row for each week in the year, a column for each day, and start to fill in the blanks. It can look amazing when done, and so obvious: all you need to do is what's on the spreadsheet, and you're all set.

Problem is, it will never happen the way you plan it. Trust me. Unless you're a professional athlete, or among the small minority who have the luxury of putting your endurance hobby ahead of other important things.

The rest of us have to deal with Real Life – jobs, family, everything else. And real life can get in the way of our extra-curricular plans, including training for the Big Event.

The answer: plan your training year in phases. You can follow three phases while building your training base to achieve your goals later in the season:

1. **Running Phase 1:** Between January and May, I tend to an average six hours training time per week. My training mix is roughly 55% running, 30% biking and 15% swimming. Running is the focus, cycling serve as great cross training, and a little swimming helps to break things up. This approach prepares me for solid Spring running races.

2. **Triathlon Phase:** June through mid-September. With a solid running base in place, transition to biking as your primary training focus beginning in June, to carry a strong running and biking base into summer triathlons. The days are warmer and longer, allowing more hours for longer training rides and outdoor swimming. The mix of swim, bike and running training should shift directly, with running and cycling almost trading direct emphasis: biking 60%, running 30%, and swimming 10%. I probably underemphasize swimming more than you should; it's a personal preference. Modify as needed, but keep cycling top priority.

3. **Running Phase 2**: Mid-September through December. With a solid triathlon training mix, and a good running season already behind you, now is the time to fine tune. Daylight is declining, there are fewer hours in the day, so I shoot to average about six hours training per week, as in the first part of the year. But the training mix, this time, is much more balanced: 50% running, 45% cycling, 5% swimming.

With these phases wrapped around your racing schedule, you can then begin to think about how your weekly training plans should look with a format called Periodization, four week cycles that increase your time and distance over the first three weeks, with the last week as a recovery week.

Periodization

I've found the best way to ramp training is in four week periods, with each week increasing in time and volume. This concept is called periodization. It allows you to concentrate only on the four-week block, and allows the body to acclimatize to increasing levels of training.

Week 1: the lowest volume week in terms of time and distance. Your workouts can blend distance, intervals, hills and recovery, but you should feel like you could be training more. Don't worry, you will soon.

Week 2: you'll add up to two hours to the week one volume. You'll take your workouts a little longer. That long run may be 30 minutes longer, that long ride might add an hour. Also you want to increase the intensity over the longer workouts.

Week 3: add another hour or two. Start focusing on not just covering more distance in more time, but these workouts should be completed with attention paid to speed. You almost want to be racing several of these workouts. The distances should begin approximating the distance you'll experience in your triathlon, e.g., 25 mile bike rides if you're preparing for an Olympic Distance race.

Week 4: your peak week. Add another hour or two, this time combining workouts. Do a 25 mile ride followed by an easy 5k run to practice what you'll experience in a race. Or swim, then hop on your bike. You're going long and simulating race conditions.

After week 4, return to week 1, which will serve as a recovery week.

Finding the Time

We all have real lives, families, jobs, and commitments that challenge our training aspirations. It can be hard to find the time to train as much as we want.

The good news is that during summer months, sunrises that approach 5am will allow you to find an early morning hour or two to train without interfering with everything else. I tend to do three or four of these early morning workouts, then one long effort, usually a training ride, on the weekend.

I train for Ironman triathlons, but you can compete in Sprint or Olympic Distance triathlons on as little as half the time. The more time you train, the faster you can be. And the more you can transition the workouts toward speed, the better off you'll be.

Workouts

During this part of the training season, start narrowing your training to core routes and distances that can be timed, repeated and compared. You want to see improvement in these routes, so track the results of each workout: time, distance and even heart rate. You want to see more distance in less time, less time for lower heart rate. All are signs you're improving.

For early mornings, I have two set bike routes – a 25 miler and a 34 miler – and I want to be faster each time I ride them. Sometimes it doesn't happen, and that's fine. But the point is, have clearly set bike training routes, and focus on improvement.

Also, pick well-measured run distances that you know well. I have a 10k, 8.5 mile, 13.1 mile loops. Find the three that work for you, and repeat, recognizing your improvement each time.

A favorite two hour early morning summer workout is what I call a 'speed brick': I ride 25 miles as fast as I can, really pushing it, then jump off the bike and run 6.2 miles, also gunning it. It's work, but highly satisfying to finish it all in less than two hours, before the work day is done. These speed bricks have made me a better triathlete, they can do the same for you.

Now you can go back to create a rough week-by-week plan and give yourself general time and distance targets. Since you know where you're headed in terms of your training and racing cycle, you'll feel more comfortable having a flexible schedule that allows you to do important things like earn a living, spend time with friends and family, and generally live a happy life.

Have Fun

And as a result, your training and racing year can then be a source of great enjoyment instead of one of anxiety. Have fun. Train Well. Race Happy.

Most important, while you're out there training, have fun. Enjoy the great weather, enjoy your improving fitness and health, enjoy being more ready than ever for your next race.

Efficiency: How Much Training Time?

What's the right amount of time/hours per week to train for a marathon, triathlon or Ironman Triathlon?

The answer is: less than you think. Perhaps a lot less than you think. And that's good news, because triathlon is really just a hobby, the kind of activity that should fit around the most important things in your life: family, friends and work.

I've tracked every minute of my training since starting endurance events in 1994. And looking back over the years, here are my benchmarks:

- First Real Triathlon season: 5 to 6 hours training hours per week
- Seasons as a top 25% or better finisher: 6 to 7 hours per week
- Seasons as a top 10% or better finisher: 7 to 8 hours per week

Simple math translates these numbers to about an hour or so of training per day. That's nothing.

Of course, my training hours per week can be more during race season and less in the off-season, but not substantially, on the whole. For examples, look at my training plans in the next chapter.

Your Mileage May Vary

These numbers may seem shocking compared to what you may read in books or magazines. For example, the Ironman website notes: "The average hours per week devoted to training for the World Championship generally fall between 18 and 22."

My reaction: impossible for mere mortals like you and me Yet I've earned a spot at the triathlon World Championships three times while training less than half the 'prescribed' time. Maybe that's not right for everyone, but my point is you don't need to dedicate insane amounts of training time to meet your goals.

Getting Started: First Real Triathlon Season

I entered my first real triathlon season as primarily a runner, with all of 18 months experience and a couple of slow marathons under my belt. My goal was to finish the Chicago Triathlon Olympic Distance event with a reasonable time and a smile on my face. To do that, I needed to improve my swim and cycling skills.

You may have a similar situation. You do not need to overdo it, however. In that first triathlon year, I trained for an average of 5 hours and 30 minutes per week. That's less than an hour per day. My average swim that year was about 30 minutes long, and my average bike ride lasted a little over one hour. Completely manageable.

Very simple: all you need to do is find that hour or less, early morning, on a lunch break, or after work, get a good workout, and return to your regularly scheduled life. And you'll do just fine in your first triathlon.

Getting Serious

For those who have some triathlon experience, maybe you're considering a longer distance, say a Half Ironman or a full Ironman. Many people balk at the thought, thinking they need to significantly increase their training time to compete at that level. I'm here to tell you, it's not necessarily true.

The year after meeting that first real triathlon goal – finish with a reasonable time and a smile – I decided to go for it all. Full Ironman triathlon, in Canada. I was excited but also more than aware of the realities of Real Life: I had a very interesting job with extensive travel, and young children at home, both of which took priority.

I had to make the most of the opportunities I had. My average swim workout increased to 45 minutes, and my average rides ranged from one to two hours, but overall the total time commitment didn't vary much. When the final tally was done, I finished not one, but two Ironman triathlons that year, averaging only 6 hours of training per week.

And when I decided to get really serious, my training bumped up to average 10 hours per week in peak season (and 6 hours otherwise), but 5am sunrises helped me train before the kids woke up and my work day began.

My running continued to be solid, so the increases came in swim time (up to one hour per session) and cycling (three hours or more early Saturday morning before breakfast). And the extra two hours (only!) per week led me to the Ironman World Championships three consecutive years.

The Key

Again, on average it all worked out to about an hour per day for a great triathlon season. You can do that. I know you can.

With less training time you need to make those workouts count. Less time and higher quality beats more time any day. You can accomplish more than you ever thought possible while maintaining the balance you want in life.

But . . .

. . . as usual, there is a little more to the story. Averages are averages; how much time does it really take, week by week, during different stages of the year.

Good question, and the answer is that, not surprisingly, my training time is less than an hour per day January through April, and the same for the late October through December. This is due to two main factors: the lack of impending races, and shorter days.

So by definition, yes, from May through September, when I'm a competitive racer – and by that I mean running like a Boston Marathon Qualifier and preparing for the Ironman World Championships in Hawaii – I can average more than an hour of training per day.

Aha, you say: Gotcha! Not quite, I will reply.

Nearly all the extra time I find for training is still what I call 'transparent'. As the sun rises earlier in summer days, so do I, taking each extra minute of daylight and translating that to additional training time. I still am at the breakfast table with the family, am at work on time, and carry on my day as any other non-triathlete would.

Long weekend training efforts follow the same principle: start the long ride at 4:30 am on a summer morning, and I can be home from a 100 mile run before 10am. Plenty of time to get my daughter to soccer, and to even handle snack duty at halftime.

Prove It

Of course, you want some more specifics. Happy to share. Remember, I have tracked every minute of training for years. (Not a bad idea for you, either. It's simple – just start a spreadsheet, or use the template on my website)

In a typical year, up until the Boston Marathon in mid-April, I will spend more time running, and cross-train biking and swimming. So far this year, my mix has been 62% run, 23% bike, and 15% swim.

I'm averaging just over six hours per week in 2007, with my longest training week, which included a 26.2 mile training marathon, just topping nine hours. Two other weeks had eight weeks of training, and the rest were seven hours or less.

This degree of training has put me in shape to run Boston reasonably well. Then the mix will change and triathlon training will pick up.

Triathlon Training Season: May through September

These are the months where my training hours will increase as I prepare for three main triathlons: Ironman USA Lake Placid in July, Chicago Triathlon in August, and Ironman Wisconsin in September.

My training mix will shift to 60% biking, 25% running and 15% swimming. My average training hours per week will increase to about 10 hours, but about every four weeks will reach 12 or 13 hours.

But let's break those really long weeks down. They are really more manageable than meets the eye. My typical 13 hour training week -- remember, this is about as intense as it gets -- will look like this:

- **Sunday**: 13 mile training run, 6:00am to 7:30am
- **Monday**: 25 mile ride, 6:00am to 7:15am
- **Tuesday**: 1 mile swim, 6:30am to 7:00am
- **Wednesday**: 40 mile ride (fast), 6 mile run, 4:45 am to 7:30am

• **Thursday**: 9 mile run 6:00am to 7:15am
• **Friday**: off or 1 mile swim, 6:30am to 7:00am
• **Saturday**: 100 mile ride, 4:30am to 9:15am then kids soccer and snack duty

Totals: 12.5 hours, 2 miles swim, 165 miles bike, 28 miles run. All done early, all bringing me to home and work without compromise to my real life for the rest of the day.

If I ever get the itch to train a little longer in a long week, but still want to keep my priorities in order, I'll swap a mid-week swim for a 40 mile bike ride, or I'll change the Sunday long-ish run to a 50 mile ride and a 6 mile run, starting at 4:30am.

Remember, the above example is the most I'd train in a given summer week. For every long week like that, there's a much shorter week to counter balance it in four week training cycle called Periodization. Each week builds upon the previous one, and after the fourth week, repeat. For example: 5, 7, 9, 11 hour training weeks in the four week cycle in summer.

Be smart with your time. Get more out of less. Your body, your boss and your family will thank you.

Balance: Training Plans, Strategy and Analysis

It's about finding balance. It's about getting the best out of yourself. It's about learning what you're capable of. It's about discovering your strengths and working on your weaknesses. It's about doing more with less time. It's your swim, bike, run life in a nutshell.

It's your training log.

It's a vital tool that can help you unlock your hidden potential. It can also help you achieve that potential despite limited time, because – let's be honest – there will never be enough time in the day to train as much as we want, while living our real, everyday lives.

Real Life

Starting as back-of-the-pack finisher eleven years ago, I wanted to find a way to improve from a novice athlete (how about a 4:47:01 debut marathon?) to eventually qualify for the Boston Marathon and the Ironman Triathlon World Championship in Kona, Hawaii.

But there were many natural obstacles: a full-time job as a tech executive, four children; in short, a full-time life that left little extra time for training. In fact, I've only been able to train an average of eight hours per week in recent years. No, that's not a typo; that's life.

To meet my goals, I had no choice but to get the maximum out of those few training hours. I needed to find a way to balance real life with my goals of improving running and triathlon performance. Sound familiar?

The simple tool I used to do it: my training log.

You can get the most out of your training by tracking the right information, doing the right analysis of your performance, making the appropriate tweaks based on that analysis, and translating those improvements into better racing.

The good news is that all it takes is a few key pieces of data after every workout, and spreadsheet calculations help you do the rest. Easy.

A Deceptively Simple Start

It all began innocently enough. On a warm summer night in August 1994, I decided to do something I'd never done before -- run a couple of miles. I liked those first two miles enough that I tried it again the next day, then again and again. I was hooked.

On a whim, I jotted down the times and distances on a piece of paper. My rationale for those notes: it would be interesting to see if I might run enough miles to actually equal a marathon distance. Little did I know that was merely the beginning.

In that 1994 training log, I entered straightforward information, very similar to what I track today. It's so simple -- intuitively, you probably already know what to include. Here's an example of my actual 2004 training log data. This is everything you'll ever need to capture about your training.

A	B	C	D	E	F	G	H	I	J	K	L
2004 Training Log											
Week	Date	Type	Distance	Time	Pace/Mile	MPH	Exercise/Route/Comment	HR	Watts	xtra	Equipment
24	6/6	Bike	31.40	1.28.37	02:49.3	21.3	LF+2V	153			SoftrideRocket
24	6/7	Run	8.50	0.57.35	06.46.5	8.9	IT			a	BrooksGlycenn
24	6/8	Bike	40.40	1:54.20	02:49.8	21.2	LFW+BG+V	149			SoftrideRocket
24	6/9	Run	8.50	0.56.22	06.37.9	9.0	BG				BrooksGlycenn
24	6/11	Bike	20.00	1:00.00	03:00.0	20.0	Computrainer/PowerCrank 20 mile flat spin		194		PowerWing/Powe
24	6/11	Swim	1.05	0.32.52	31.16.1	1.9					5S
24	6/12	Bike	30.70	1.33.00	03:01.8	19.8	low HR spin V+LF+V	133			SoftrideRocket
25	6/13	Run	13.10	1.22.46	06.19.1	9.5	North Shore Half Marathon				BrooksRacerST
25	6/14	Bike	30.44	1:26.44	02:51.0	21.1	LF+V+	145			SoftrideRocket
25	6/15	Bike	30.38	1.25.04	02:48.0	21.4	LF+V+	152			SoftrideRocket
25	6/15	Swim	0.99	0:31.10	31:20.5	1.9				xa	5S
25	6/16	Run	3.50	0.26.30	07.34.3	7.9	Easy run in Dallas				BrooksGlycerin
25	6/17	Bike	27.34	1:17.02	02:49.1	21.3	LF rain	149			SoftrideRocket
25	6/18	Swim	0.97	0.30.02	31.00.1	1.9					5S

- Week and Date: noting the Week will allow you to aggregate training totals later; I start my weeks on Sunday as a psychological boost. This way it's possible to start the week with a long training effort, as opposed to saving it all up for the end of a more traditional week that ends with Sunday.
- Type: For type of activity, list Swim, Bike or Run – simple enough, but this will be key to totaling your workouts and seeing important patterns such as training mix and comparative performance by discipline
- Distance and Time: The basics of your workout; don't worry if you don't have exact information, use estimates if necessary

- Pace/Mile and Miles Per Hour: these data can be simply calculated with a formula to gauge performance versus perceived effort over similar workouts
- Exercise/Route/Comment: include short notes about your workout, route, conditions, anything that's noteworthy, should you choose to compare against other similar workouts later
- Heart Rate: I'm not a slave to heart rate training, but occasionally, I will wear a heart rate monitor to manage training effort. Having this information allows you to compare similar workouts on similar routes; lower HR/MPH over time indicates you're improving
- Watts: When I ride CompuTrainer indoors for winter training, which tends to be six months per year, I track wattage. In doing so, I look for higher watts relative to heart rate as an indicator that I'm training better.
- xtra: I keep simple notes about light weight work (I use an 'x' for exercise) and abdominal work (an 'a')
- Equipment: I enter the equipment I use so I can tell when it's time to change shoes (roughly 300 miles per pair), or see how much time I'm using certain equipment, e.g. riding indoors on CompuTrainer vs. outdoors on my Softride Rocket.
- Other fields: It's possible to enter much more information, but be careful to avoid data overkill. I loosely track body weight, but not much else.

It's that simple. You could stop there, not do further analysis of your training, and this would still be a useful tool.

Having this baseline information helped me qualify for the Boston Marathon in 1995. My big challenge: knock a full minute per mile off of my previous best marathon time. I became totally focused on driving myself to that faster level. I aimed my workouts toward speedier, quality miles, looking forward to entering the better results in my training log each time.

In a way, the training log, this simple spreadsheet, had become my master and coach. I knew the target I needed to reach, I was accountable for it, and I strove to get there and beyond in each workout.

In October 1995, I ran the Chicago Marathon in 3:14:28, qualifying for Boston. The bigger deal: having knocked 85 minutes off my debut marathon time in one year, largely because of unrelenting focus on the numbers in my training log.

But focusing on the raw data is only the beginning. The fun starts next.

Finding the Story Behind The Numbers

The magic comes in the way you analyze the information in your training log. There's a story in the data, a story about you, how you train, what you're capable of, what you prefer, what you avoid, and what your strengths and weaknesses are.

The plot can thicken as you assess changes in progress, performance and fitness over time as different variables change, e.g., distance, effort, heart rate, watts. By analyzing your training data you can crack the code to find your opportunities to improve. And the code covers the gamut – weekly totals, training mix, annual totals, comparing previous years, and equipment.

All it takes is a few simple Microsoft Excel calculations and Pivot Tables to convert the data entered in your training log into key insights about how you train.

Weekly Totals

While preparing for my first Ironman triathlon in 1997, I diligently read as much training material as possible. One of the most valuable things I learned was the concept of periodization, four week cycles building to greater training time, followed by a rest week, then the cycle began again. This intuitively made sense; take your body to a new level, ease off to recover, then go even higher.

On paper, training plans built on the principle of periodization looked great. But real life got in the way, often robbing precious training time, and shattering hopes of staying on the textbook schedule I had planned. And it's still the same, year after year. To counterbalance these time challenges, I need a guide to keep me on track.

This is where the Weekly Totals analysis in my training log comes in. I've learned to take distractions as they come, and to try to rough out weekly training that approximates periodization. A Pivot Table calculates the raw data, and a chart is linked to the weekly totals. Seeing my weekly training in chart form provides a visual to tell me if I'm on track.

2004 Hours Per Week

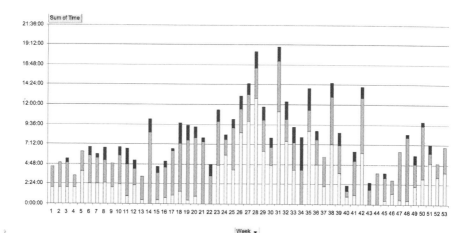

The above chart captures my 2004 training and racing year, which averaged just over eight training hours per week. As you can see, some weeks exceeded ten hours (several of those weeks included marathons or Ironman races), but most are under eight hours. You can see the blocks of time that approximated periodization. Not strictly by the book, but good enough to lead to a 10:12:22 Ironman personal best in Lake Placid in week 31.

These weekly training totals might look low compared to the averages tossed around in triathlon forums, but I contend that total hours mean far less than the quality of training in those hours. It's quality, not quantity. You want to make sure the combination of the daily workouts and the weekly totals is projecting you forward. That's your main focus, having great training hours, not just accumulating time.

Year-to-Date Summary

While the weekly picture of your training provides ongoing perspective, a Year-To-Date Summary analysis tells you what you've accomplished in total for the year – time, distance, averages by discipline. More importantly, it gives you insight into what you need to change. Here's my 2005 year-to-date summary, as of 4/25/05.

2005	Type ▾			
Data ▾	Bike	Run	Swim	Grand Total
Sum of Distance	999.27	337.46	17.06	1,353.79
Sum of Time	47:49:02	42:55:23	8:59:36	99:44:01
Count of Type	38	32	16	86
Avg Dist/Exercise	26.30	10.55	1.07	15.74
Avg Time/Exercise	1:15:30	1:20:29	0:33:44	1:09:35
Avg Time/mile	02:52.3	07:37.9	31:37.9	04:25.2
Time/day	0:25:10	0:22.35	0:04:44	0:52:29
Time/week	2:56:10	2:38:08	0:33:08	6:07:26
Dist/week	61.36	20.72	1.05	83.13

This snapshot is interesting by itself, but gains more power when compared with the same picture from previous years. You want to look for differences, improvements, and weaknesses to work on. Here's my full year summary for 2004.

2004	Type ▾			
Data ▾	Bike	Run	Swim	Grand Total
Sum of Distance	3,452.69	1,632.70	101.64	5,187.03
Sum of Time	168:43:20	200:52:00	53:00:26	422:35:46
Count of Type	127	177	88	392
Avg Dist/Exercise	27.19	9.22	1.16	13.23
Avg Time/Exercise	1:19:43	1:08:05	0:36:08	1:04:41
Avg Time/mile	02:55.9	07:22.9	31:17.4	04:53.3
Time/day	0:27:44	0:33:01	0:08:43	1:09:28
Time/week	3:14:09	3:51:08	1:01:00	8:06:16
Dist/week	66.22	31.31	1.95	99.48

Although my 2005 total hours per week are lower that I'd prefer – life getting in the way again – there are several good things this training log summary tells me. It says that my training mix is close to where I'd like it, at least for the first part of the year – heavier on biking, although certainly light on swimming. The average times per mile are among the best I've seen by April -- particularly in cycling – leading to a confidence boost compared to other years. My distances per week are lower than they will be in summer, obviously, but not too bad, except for the swimming again.

All in all, not bad for six hours per week in 2005. Again, an extra benefit comes from being able to compare this analysis with the same period for previous years. You want to make sure you're not repeating mistakes, but instead are repeating good patterns from the past.

Training Mix

Speaking of making mistakes from the past, I was an expert at it, until I saw the light, in the data.

I had been training for and competing in Ironman races since 1997. By the end of 2001, I had improved somewhat, but there seemed to be an impossible gap between what I thought was the best I could do and what seemed required to qualify for Kona. The gap, in my estimation, was at least 40 minutes in an Ironman race. I had to do something different. But what?

Once I posed the question, no serious scrutiny was necessary. I had to look no further than at a sum-total table in my training log that summarized time by discipline, per year. The simple table of annual totals told the story.

Hours	Swim	Bike	Run	Total
1994	0:00:00	0:00:00	21:52:30	21:52:30
1995	7:38:37	17:24:14	168:33:04	193:35:54
1996	27:10:57	55:33:16	205:10:19	287:54:32
1997	39:41:19	101:38:28	165:48:34	307:08:21
1998	21:36:45	147:32:39	147:12:06	316:21:30
1999	14:45:01	119:14:11	175:21:31	309:20:43
2000	9:03:52	85:49:19	184:41:38	279:34:49
2001	57:36:28	130:40:23	187:16:16	375:33:07
2002	78:27:19	196:47:00	167:55:26	443:09:45
2003	44:19:34	179:58:59	168:06:27	392:25:00
2004	53:00:26	168:43:20	200:52:00	422:35:46
2005	8:59:36	47:49:02	42:55:23	99:44:01
Total	362:19:54	1251:10:51	1835:45:14	3449:15:59

The answer was obvious. In 2001 I was running 50% of the time, biking 35% of the time, and swimming 15% of the time. You can guess two things from these numbers: I preferred running, and I was not a particularly good cyclist or swimmer in Ironman races. I was stuck in a comfort zone. A zone that was perfectly fine if I never wanted to improve, but one that needed to change rapidly if I wanted to get to Kona.

I made a dramatic shift in the first seven months of 2002. Whenever possible, I was on the bike. Long rides, intervals, hills, whatever. I needed to spend more time improving on the bike. That was my focus, and my training mix changed accordingly.

The shift paid off. By the time I got to Ironman Lake Placid in July, I was more than ready for the hills, and more ready than I'd ever been to run a marathon after a 112 mile bike ride. My training log dictated the change, I followed the guide, and I got what I wanted: my first Kona slot.

To this day, I keep a close eye on training mix. Even early in the year, when it's easy to let things slip, and when it's easy to skip an indoor ride in favor of a preferred outdoor run. My training log has been reminding me to not stray, with a simple pie chart that shows the training mix. It keeps me honest. It says: keep the balance.

Equipment

The last piece of information I analyze is something that might be considered an afterthought: equipment. I first started tracking time and distance with regard to shoes, and later extended it to include everything – bikes, pools, etc.

Again, it's as simple as creating a Pivot Table to capture the data from your training log entries. To that, I've added calculations to show pace and speed for each. Below is an excerpt of my 2004 Equipment Training log.

I use this information to tell me when to change shoes (around 300 miles per pair), when to spend more time riding outdoors compared to indoors (I like a 1/3 indoor, 2/3 outdoor mix for the entire year), etc. Also, I can compare totals and averages against previous years to know if I'm performing better on certain things, or what needs to improve.

How much is too much?

Can you have too much information in your training log? You bet. It's tempting, and I've done it. Big mistake.

	A	B	C	D	E
1	2004 Equipment				
2	Equipment ▼	Data ▼	Total	Pace/mile	Avg
3	5S	Sum of Time	42:13:59		
4		Sum of Distance	81.07	0:31:15	per mile
5		Count of Distance	75	1.08	per swim
6	BrooksAdrenalineGTS5	Sum of Time	19:13:13		
7		Sum of Distance	155.50	0:07:25	per mile
8		Count of Distance	15	10.37	per run
9	PowerWing/PowerCranks/CT	Sum of Time	56:30:40		1:00:00
10		Sum of Distance	1,111.12	0:03:03	19.7 mpl
11		Count of Distance	69	16.10	per ride
12	BrooksAdrenalineGTS5a	Sum of Time	45:09:58		
13		Sum of Distance	363.9	0:07:27	per mile
14		Count of Distance	43.0	8.46	per run
15	IronmanWetsuitsStealth	Sum of Time	3:56:43		
16		Sum of Distance	8.0	0:29:31	per mile
17		Count of Distance	6.0	1.34	per swim
18	SoftrideRocket	Sum of Time	108:53:42		1:00:00
19		Sum of Distance	2,272.6	0:02:53	20.9 mpl
20		Count of Distance	54.0	42.08	per ride
21	BrooksAdrenalineGTS5b	Sum of Time	33:47:30		
22		Sum of Distance	268.3	0:07:33	per mile
23		Count of Distance	27.0	9.94	per run
24	BrooksAdrenalineASB	Sum of Time	3:11:28		

I got so obsessed about training data in the late 1990s that at one point I had broken each main running route into ten different segments, and entered time and heart rate for each segment. I then plotted a regression of heart rate versus speed for each segment. This led me to the point that I could almost predict the finishing time of a 20 mile run based on my heart rate after the first mile.

Frankly, it was too much information. I found myself more tied up in knots about the data, and less about the workouts. Looking back, I knew a great deal about the metrics of my training, but all that did little to improve my training or racing. I had all the data in the world, but was stuck in a rut. So I went back to the basics, using the primary data described above. This simple data has served me well, and can serve you well, too.

When Time Isn't On Your Side

It's great when you have the time you want, relatively speaking, and are able to carry out your training plans in a way that translates to a good daily, weekly and annual balance. But sometimes, life throws a curve or two that calls for you to spend less time training than you'd like. Never mind that there are exciting races on the calendar, never mind that they come at you before you're ready.

This past winter and spring has been a classic example of this, as I looked forward to Ironman Arizona and the Boston Marathon. Consuming work and important family activities, not to mention another icy cold, windy Chicago winter, drove my training time to lower levels than I wanted.

These challenges forced me to wedge the absolute most out of minimal training in order to still race well in April. I looked at previous year training logs and borrowed the best workouts, the ones that seemed to make me improve the fastest.

While my weekly training hours were low, averaging close to only six hours per week, consistently the daily detail told me that those hours were more productive than ever, and the annual averages confirmed that, relative to previous solid years.

Weekly Hours

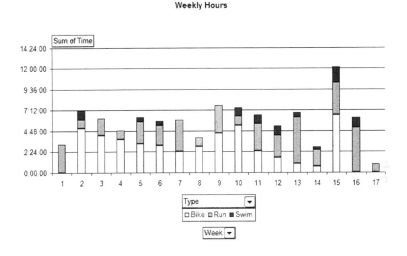

The results: on April 9, I completed Ironman Arizona in 10:36:05, my third best Ironman ever (I've done 24 so far); a week later, I ran the Boston Marathon in 3:02:24, my second best time in ten races there.

I can't say that running these two races on an average of six hours per week training is for everybody. But I can say with confidence that I would not have performed so well without being able to apply lessons from the past to get the most out of training a very limited timeframe. Again, my training log – past and present -- served as a guide that took me to solid race performances.

Used right, your training log can do the same for you.

You as Science Experiment

Pull all the pieces together – the data you enter after every workout, and the calculations and tables that can be generated quickly – and there's so much to learn about your training. It's as if you are your own personal science experiment.

Whether it's comparing speed vs. heart rate, comparing time trials over similar courses, assessing how well you perform in winter vs. summer over multiple years, or comparing year over year performance, your training log can provide everything you need.

Remember: keep it simple. You don't need very much information, but you can take it a long way. Your training log can tell you things that an endless series of triathlon books and articles will never reveal – the core truth about your training strengths, weaknesses, opportunities for improvement.

It's all there for you. Every workout is another piece of information that can take you closer to your goals. Save the data. Let your training log do the heavy lifting. Analyze changes over time, the good and the bad.

The more you save and analyze, the better you will know yourself and the more you will have opportunities to race better, to unlock your potential, to meet and even exceed your racing goals. And in that equation, hopefully you will also find balance, balance that allows you to live your life fully, in an optimal blend of work, friends, family, training, and of course, racing.

Execution:
Everything Else You Need To Know

At each Ironman race these days – or Half Ironman, Olympic Distance, or even Sprint races for that matter – hundreds or more of the athletes are tackling triathlon for the first time.

And they all have the same questions: What do I need to take? What do I do when I get there? What should I expect? What do I need to carry? What might go wrong? How do I deal with it?

It can seem overwhelming. So much to do, so much to remember.

Let me simplify it for you.

Do what you or your coach think is right to get you to the point where you're ready to race, ready to cover the distance. I'll help you with the rest – what to expect and what to do – from packing for your trip to crossing the finish line:

*   What to Take
*   Assembly Once You Get There
*   Bike Check-in
*   Planning Nutrition
*   Race Morning – Final Preparations
*   The Race: Swim, Transition, Bike, Transition, Run
*   Finishing With a Smile

It takes a few races to get it all figured out, believe me. With 29 Ironman finishes over the last nine years, I think I can pretty well answer many of those questions for rookies, and even for those that have done more than one race, but are still looking for the right combination.

This article is mainly for the Ironman triathlete, but all principles apply in most ways to shorter triathlons as well.

What to Take

There are so many things to pack or, put another way, so many things to potentially forget. And yes, I have forgotten many different things over the years.

But I have learned not to panic, for a simple reason: even if you forgot everything, you still could buy just about all of it at the race merchandise area. Just knowing you have that backstop should make your packing less worrisome.

Because I'll tell you right now: you will forget something, probably a few somethings. Don't worry. Wetsuits, Bikes, components, nutrition, just about everything but running shoes (which you can buy at a sporting goods store) can typically be found on site.

But to remember to bring the right things, here's the approach: pre-pack your transition bags.

Create five piles in the packing room, one each for Prerace, Swim, Bike, Run, Nutrition. As you grab items from your closet, bags, car, wherever, lay them in the appropriate piles.

My basics are:
- Prerace: clothes to wear to/from transition – jacket and sweatpants, and what I'll wear during the entire race – bike shirt, tri-shorts, timing chip and strap
- Swim: wetsuit, goggles, sunscreen, body glide, extra swim cap, swimsuit
- Bike: helmet, sunglasses, bike shoes, gloves, race belt, socks, arm warmers
- Run: hat, shoes, extra race belt, socks, and sunglasses if you need them
- Nutrition/other: bring the essentials you are sure you won't find on the race site. A favorite gel, certain salt tablets or pain reliever, perhaps. Have a small plastic container – I prefer a 35mm film holder – to hold salt and ibuprofen on the bike.

Place the contents into five bags, labeled accordingly, and drop them in your suitcase. For me, one of those bags is an athletic bag, which I later use to carry things to/from transition.

Packing the bike can be intimidating. After dialing in your perfect position, the last thing you want to do is disassemble it. To restore your bike to that perfect position later, use black electrical tape to mark measurements. Seat post, handlebars, anything that moves or is removed should have a tape mark. Do that, and you can return to your perfect dialed-in position when you reassemble your bike.

So you're not scrambling on race day, pack your saddle bag in advance with everything you'll need before the trip. Replacement tube or tire, glue if necessary, co2 adapter (buy co2 on site), disc wheel air adapter (if necessary), hex tool, extra contact lenses (yes, you might need them).

Pressing bike pieces inside a tight transport case is a scary concept. To avoid friction in transit, wrap the frame and anything else that might have contact in bubble wrap or some other protective material. I use several Velcro straps use to secure the protection in place. And knowing how bike cases can be tossed around behind airline counters, I've added Velcro on the outside of the case itself to further secure the contents.

Follow these steps, and you should have just about everything you need with you when you arrive at the race registration.

Assembly

Unpack soon after arriving to make sure you brought everything, or more important, to find out if you forgot anything. Time flies surprisingly fast once you get to the race city, and if you need something – I usually do, CO2 cartridges and GU at a minimum – you need to find out early.

It's especially important to get your bike assembled and tested right away. If a screw gets stripped or a tire won't inflate, you want to know that as soon as possible. There's nothing worse than finding out your bike stem needs to be replaced right before bike check-in, and then scrambling to find the right size, shape, whatever. Yes, it's happened to me, and yes, I've panicked when the right part couldn't be found. You don't want that to happen to you.

After you get your race transition bags at registration, lay them out, and match the Swim, Bike, Run bags you had packed earlier. It's as simple as transferring the contents – you've already pre-packed your transition bags. Again, if you forgot anything, you'll find out at this time, and have the opportunity to buy what's missing.

An important note about bib numbers and race belts. Bib numbers can be flimsy, can tear, and can fly off during the race. And losing your number can mean a penalty (silly rule, but I've seen it enforced). My secret to avoiding all this: black electrical tape. Put black electrical tape over the top two holes of your bib number, front and back. This more than doubles the reinforcement. Then poke the pin on your race belt through the electrical tape to secure the bib number. The electrical tape holds perfectly. I've never lost a bib number on the course with this method.

Bike Check-In

In my early races, I remember being particularly worried that I'd forgotten something essential on the day of bike and transition bag check-in the day before the race. I'd check and recheck the bags, and still be nervous.

But there's no reason for concern. At most races, you have access to your bags race morning, and if you forget anything, you can add it then. Again, relax.

Just make sure you've got the basics in the bags: bib number, helmet, bike shoes, running shoes. If you swim in your tri-outfit, you can finish the race with just those items. Everything else – sunglasses, gloves, socks, hat – extra. If you have it there, perfect. If you forgot, don't sweat it.

It's pretty easy to find bikes belonging to some of the triathlon rookies at any race. How to spot them? Easy. Three water bottles already in cages on the bike, and nutrition already put in place. PowerBar squares sticking to the top tube of some bikes, an open invitation for bugs. Nasty.

Believe me, after exposure to a hot day and a cool night, that stuff will not be appealing on race day. Keep your nutrition and bottles with you overnight, and put them in place on race morning.

I had a string of triathlons that involved rain the night before the race, and now bring plastic trash bags to put over handlebars and the seat if the forecast suggests a wet night. Covering the handlebars means a dry surface to tape nutrition (all my GU slipped off wet handlebars in transition at one race). Some people cover their chain, too. Some cover the entire bike. That's overkill for me, but it's up to you.

After that, you'll have nothing to do except relax and think about the nutrition and hydration you'll carry the following day.

Planning Race Nutrition

Planning your hydration and nutrition needs for an Ironman can be tricky. Too much and you'll feel sick, too little and you'll bonk. And then there's the worry about how to get enough calories during the day. I've seen sandwiches strapped to handlebars. I've ridden with riders whose watches beeped every fifteen minutes telling them to eat more fig bars. I've seen athletes load up a Camelback to carry fluid with them on the bike and the same athletes stop in their tracks at Special Needs to reload another bladder of fluid.

It all seems like so much work. It has to be simpler.

It took me many races of trial and error to find the right mix. What I ended up with may be a formula that can be applied to your needs, though the specific ingredients might change.

After many races, I found that about about 2500 to 3000 calories was my optimal calorie count on the bike. Simply, that translates to about 250 calories every 10 miles on the bike. This amount not only keeps me fueled for the bike, but also prepares me for the run. So that is my target. Practice caloric intake on your long training rides to find the level right for you.

In terms of how to get those calories, here's what I came up with:

- 800 calories GU: 8 packets, 100 calories each, Plain is the preferred flavor
- 920 calories PowerBars: 4 chocolate PowerBars,
- 300 calories: Bananas: grab 6 bananas at aid stations
- 750 calories Gatorade: take at least 5 bottles Gatorade, one every other aid station, 5 x 125 calories

Race Morning: Final Preparations

My race morning routine is simple.

First, you can arrive terrifyingly early. Don't. As long as you can get there an hour before the race, you're fine. Arrive two hours early, and you've added anxiety time. Relax.

Second, get the bike ready:

- Tape the 8 GU gels to aerobars, four on each side
- Place four PowerBars in Profile-Design Velcro pouch on the top of my Softride beam
- Put the plastic container (35mm film) container with ibuprofen and sodium in the pouch
- Insert one water bottle in bottle cage (with regular aid stations, I see no reason to carry more)
- Check the tires
- Put White Lightning on the chain
- Set the bike computer distance and time setting to zero

Next, I go to transition area and make sure at least helmet, bike shoes, bib number and running shoes are in the bags. That's the minimum you need, if you forgot anything.

After that. Relax, breathe deep, and look forward to a fun day of endurance. Now all you have to do is travel 140.6 miles (or the distance of your triathlon). Again, don't worry. Plenty of time -- you've got 17 hours to do it.

Swim

In my experience, not too much can go terribly wrong in the swim. You get through it, either quickly, or not. How fast you go depends on your training.

How much physical contact you endure depends on where you start. I've tried starting everywhere: at the rear, up front, inside on the 'line', outside. There will be contact no matter where you start.

Someone will inadvertently kick you. You will accidentally bump into someone else. It may feel violent, but no one wants to hurt anyone. Do not take it personally. Know that the person who almost knocked your goggles off really wished that didn't happen, sorry. Relax.

If you start at the rear and you're willing to wait about 30 seconds after the cannon goes off, it can be a fairly breezy swim. The benefit is a complete draft of all swimmers in front of you; the downside may be that you need to navigate around many people.

Most of the time, I hope to start on the side, near the front, with the hope that it will not be congested. Except that hundreds of athletes also seem to have the same idea. So the sides tend to be pretty densely packed.

For the rookie who's not an expert swimmer, relax at the swim start, let others start ahead of you, and do your best to swim in a straight line. If you lose five or ten minutes on a slow swim, you can make it up on the bike or run.

For the rookies who are fast swimmers, I envy you. Go to the front, swim well, and enjoy being in front of most of the athletes for a while. Say hi to me when I pass you on the bike.

Swim to Bike Transition

I am usually disoriented coming out of the water. It's not easy to immediately adjust to land after more than an hour bobbing and weaving through the water. Take your time exiting the water, and begin running to transition. Volunteers may be there to help remove your wetsuit. After that, other volunteers will help you find your transition bag. Thank them for helping you.

Find a seat, put on your helmet, bib number, socks and shoes. Make sure debris is off your feet first, because you may choose to run in those socks later. Decide if you want to take arm warmers. My advice: when in doubt, be comfortable. I usually wear arm warmers on the bike, knowing I might discard them later. And I'm usually glad I have them.

Get sunscreen before you head out to get your bike. Volunteers will slather it on you in fifteen seconds. Skip that step, and you will be explaining strange sunburn patterns to your family later.

Bike

For me, the first few hours on the bike are perhaps the most enjoyable part of the Ironman. You feel fresh, you feel fast, people are in good moods. And then there's the scenery. Every course has wonderful scenery, in its own way. It's one of the reasons we race.

Can something go wrong on your bike ride, the one you prepared so diligently for? Sure. Be prepared for it, not afraid.

Something different seems to happen to me in every race. I've had flat tires in Austria and in the US. I've had contact lenses fly out of my eyes on the bike in Canada and in Germany. More than once I've pulled my bike out of transition, only to see 1000 calories of nutrition fly off the bike onto the street (I've learned a thing or two about securing nutrition in place as a result).

The point is, expect the unexpected, and embrace it as part of the triathlon experience. Being a triathlete is about overcoming obstacles. Unexpected problems included.

I saw several people on the side of the road on the Ironman Arizona 2006 bike course with flat tires or some other bike mechanical problem. More than a few of them had looks of deep despair, head in hands. They were looks of shattered dreams. And at the moment, they may have been. But there are other chances, other races. I've done enough races to know that a single race is never the definitive one. Do what you can to get back on the course, and finish.

If you get a flat tire, try to change it. I flew all the way to Austria, in hope of a fast race in 2001, only to flat on the first loop. I lost 10 minutes changing the flat, and that wasn't too bad. I didn't let it kill my day.

In Ironman USA Lake Placid 2005, two of the three screws on my cycling shoe cleat fell out. I stropped to try to fix it to no avail, then rode the last 25 miles gingerly with a loose cleat. It cost me many precious minutes (and I missed a Kona slot by one minute), but I've decided life is too short to worry about things that happen. They do. You'll be fine.

If you need to wait for race support for help, it could take a long time. If that happens, don't get upset, just change your goal. A friend waited 45 minutes waiting for assistance at Ironman Idaho, after which he found himself almost completely at the rear of all athletes. So he changed the challenge. He would now try to see how many people he could pass for the remainder of the bike ride. He must have passed more than 1000 people, and was satisfied with that.

Executing the bike nutrition plan is about as simple as putting it together. Remember, your exact nutrition may vary, but the concept is the same – balanced calorie input throughout your ride. Here's the timing. Simple.

- GU: Take a GU sometime within every 10 mile segment. That gets you to 80 miles. Easy to remember, each time you see a mile marker with a zero, eat a GU.
- PowerBar: Eat a PowerBar within every 25 mile segment. Yes, this overlaps with GU somewhat, but that's not a problem. I usually eat them between miles 15 and 20, 40 and 45, and 65 and 70. The last one depends on how I'm feeling late in the ride.
- Gatorade: it's essential to always have one with you on the bike. Grab one each aid station and put it in a bottle cage.
- Water: I also grab a water bottle, but try to swig half of it then toss it by the end of the aid station. With aid stations every 10 miles, I can't come up with a reason to carry more than one bottle.
- Bananas: it's unpredictable which aid stations will have them, so I grab one each time I see it. Some races do not have bananas, and you might have to substitute. Just make sure you grab those 300 calories somewhere.
- Salt/Ibuprofen: I took a salt tablet and an ibuprofen tablet every 30 miles. Read directions to make sure your ibuprofen dose is appropriate.

I don't use special needs bags on the bike or run. I decided long ago it's not worth the hassle. Everything I need is on the bike or at aid stations. I think the same is true for most athletes. Not to mention my experience is that getting your bag in a timely manner tends to be a challenge, and most of the time what you included in the bag is not appealing when you actually get it.

Bike To Run Transition

By the time you finish the bike, you're feeling ready to run. At least mentally. Ready to run in the sense that you're ready to not ride anymore, at a minimum.

Reality will set in when you hop off the bike, give it to a waiting volunteer, and begin to head towards transition. Those first few steps after 112 miles are quite a surprise. You feel like you almost can't move forward. Your first thought may be: I don't think I can 26.2 miles now.

Rest assured that in about 30 seconds, you'll feel better. Keep running, pick up your bag, and get to the change tent. By the time you get your running shoes and hat on, you'll feel surprisingly ready to run. Get more sunscreen, acknowledge the cheers of the spectators on the railing, and head out onto the run course.

Run

In the same way you might get a flat tire on the run, you may physically flat on the run. Cramps, bad patches, tough times. For the Ironman rookie, this might be the longest continuous timeframe you've ever moved your body forward. It may want to give out soon. But know that sometimes it can get better after it gets worse. Keep moving forward, keep hydrating and drinking.

Most aid stations, usually only one mile apart, have water, cola, Gatorade, chicken broth, oranges, bananas, pretzels, GU and ice. Train with these, and you'll need nothing more on race day.

The run hydration/nutrition plan is even simpler than on the bike, because you don't need to carry anything. I've worked out similar 'rules' for consistency, including:

- Two cups of cola with ice at least every other aid station. Cola provides sugar, caffeine and sodium. That's about 50 calories x 13 = 650 calories
- If bearable, GU every 4 miles. That's about 600 calories if you get them all.
- When the chicken broth is available, take it. It's Go Juice. High levels of sodium will make you feel better, guaranteed. Though the mix of cola and broth in your stomach might not feel the best.

At Ironman Arizona, because of the very dry air, I found myself needing to have cola at every aid station. Do what you need to do. The only thing to avoid is getting behind on your hydration or nutrition. Try to keep up.

And run as the best you can, at least at a pace that you can sustain for a few hours. If you need to walk a hill or two, do it. Walk the aid stations. Keep moving forward. Nothing will keep you from your Ironman finish. It's just a matter of time now.

Finish

You've trained all year to get there. You've raced all day to get there. Enjoy the moments in the final meters of the finish line chute. Let others enjoy their moment, too. Don't race someone to the finish line, unless you think a Kona slot is on the line. Let the racer in front of you get a finish line photo to cherish. Then go get your own.

Cross the line, smile for the camera, and consider yourself a member of the club. You are an Ironman.

Finish Line

I hope this Book provides the information you need to have a great Ironman race. If there are some questions that still need answers, feel free to contact me via my website, www.RunTri.com.

There is no experience like racing and finishing the Ironman Triathlon. But the experience getting there can be every bit as rewarding, too.

Good luck in your quest for Kona.

Appendix 1:

Kona Qualifying Year 1:

Training Plan Details

Date	Type	Dist	Time	Pace	MPH	Exercise	HR	Watts	Wts	Shoes
1/1	Bike	15.00	0:45:00	03:00.0	20.0	PS1B 3x3xhigh	153	212	xa	CT
1/1	Run	2.63	0:30:00	11:24.4	5.3	P1L7 brick	153			TM
1/2	Swim	1.79	1:00:20	33:42.3	1.8				a	5S
1/2	Bike	23.63	1:25:00	03:35.8	16.7	TDF15/2	150	196		CT
1/3	Swim	1.79	1:00:16	33:40.4	1.8				aPilates	5S
1/4	Bike	20.00	1:02:26	03:07.3	19.2	2x6(+2)x2.5'	148	197	a	CT
1/4	Swim	1.85	1:00:11	32:35.5	1.8	excellent				5S
1/5	Run	11.60	1:25:00	07:19.7	8.2	JP to HP route			aSkating	NXT
1/6	Bike	56.00	2:55:56	03:08.5	19.1	IMNZ lap 1	150	181	xa	CT
1/7									a	
1/8	Swim	1.85	0:59:59	32:29.0	1.8	better			xas	5S
1/8	Bike	25.80	1:15:00	02:54.4	20.6	3x6x2.5' RI 20" 15'w/u	153	214		CT
1/9	Run	9.10	0:59:14	06:30.5	9.2	BT			xa	NXT
1/10	Bike	112.00	5:33:59	02:58.9	20.1	IMNZ	151	197	xa	CT
1/11						60' skating				
1/12	Run	14.02	1:42:44	07:19.7	8.2	JP to HP route				NXT
1/13	Bike	20.10	1:00:00	02:59.1	20.1		150	197	skating	CT
1/14						rest				
1/15	Bike	15.80	0:50:00	03:09.9	19.0	spin	135	175		CT
1/15	Swim	1.85	1:01:08	33:06.4	1.8				xas	5S
1/16	Swim	1.82	1:00:48	33:26.4	1.8				xa	5S
1/17	Swim	1.88	1:00:48	32:25.6	1.9				xas	5S
1/18	Bike	56.00	2:42:42	02:54.3	20.7	IMNZ lap 1	155	216		CT
1/18	Run	1.70	0:17:12	10:07.1	5.9	treadmill brick easy	138			TM
1/19	Run	11.10	1:20:35	07:15.6	8.3	JP route HP				NXT
1/20	Run	8.50	1:00:42	07:08.5	8.4	BG; 40% snow/ice			a	NXT
1/21	Swim	1.99	1:05:15	32:48.7	1.8				xa	5S
1/21	Bike	24.00	1:10:00	02:55.0	20.6	1to6to1 ladder L1 2' RI	150	210		CT
1/21	Run	4.87	0:40:00	08:12.8	7.3	flat treadmill brick	144			NXT2
1/22	Swim	1.85	0:59:08	32:01.4	1.9				xas	5S
1/22	Bike	21.40	1:05:00	03:02.2	19.8	easy CT flat	137	182		CT
1/23	Run	13.10	1:26:34	06:36.5	9.1	HM loop; slick last 3			xa	NXT2
1/24	Swim	1.59	0:50:20	31:38.3	1.9				xa	5S
1/24	Bike	77.65	4:00:00	03:05.4	19.4	IMNZ; struggle through hour 2	140	184		CT
1/25	Run	1.50	0:15:00	10:00.0	6.0	easy brick after ride				NXT2
1/25	Swim	1.93	1:01:25	31:47.5	1.9				xas	5S
1/26	Run	18.00	2:10:47	07:15.9	8.3		153			NXT2
1/27	Bike	27.00	1:30	03:20.0	18.0	estimate; outdoor ride			xa	SR
1/28	Bike	20.54	1:00:00	02:55.3	20.5	4-8-12-8-4 ladder	153	209		CT
1/28	Run	4.66	0:40:00	08:35.0	7.0	brick run	142			TM
1/29	Swim	1.90	1:00:57	32:01.3	1.9	first 1800 in 31:34			as	5S
1/30	Swim	0.82	0:26:19	31:56.6	1.9				xas	5S
1/31						bronchitis, etc.				
2/1						bronchitis, etc.				
2/2	Bike	16.80	1:00:00	03:34.3	16.8	recovery spin	120	130	xa	CT
2/3	Run	9.10	1:10:53	07:47.4	7.7		157			NXT2
2/4	Swim	0.77	0:25:22	33:04.2	1.8					5S
2/4	Bike	20.00	1:00:00	03:00.0	20.0	15 12 10 ladder	153	203	x	CT
2/5	Swim	1.82	1:00:54	33:29.7	1.8				xas	5S
2/5	Run	4.02	0:45:00	11:11.6	5.4	P1L9 hills 5.4 mph 8-12% grade	160			NXT2
2/6	Swim	1.90	1:01:26	32:16.5	1.9	BT loop			xas	5S
2/6	Run	9.10	1:04:25	07:04.7	8.5					NXT2
2/7	Bike	40.40	2:00:00	02:58.2	20.2	IMNZ loop 40.4	150	197		CT
2/8	Swim	1.88	1:00:15	32:08.0	1.9				xa	5S
2/9	Run	20.65	2:35:04	07:30.6	8.0	HM+				NXT2
2/9	Bike	19.00	1:00:00	03:09.5	19.0	Fort Sheridan outside			xa	SR

Week	Date	Type	Dist	Time	Pace	MPH	Exercise	HR	Watts	Wts	Shoes
7	2/12	Bike	23.00	1:10:00	03:02.6	19.7	10' 5x5' Ladder 3' RI	148	197		CT
7	2/13	Swim	1.85	1:00:12	32:36.0	1.8				s	5S
7	2/13	Run	9.10	1:04:00	07:02.0	8.5					NXT2
7	2/14						exhausted				
7	2/15	Swim	1.88	1:01:59	33:03.5	1.8	exhausted, several breaks			xas	5S
7	2/15	Bike	6.69	0:20:00	02:59.4	20.1	easy spin	144	193		CT
7	2/16	Run	26.20	3:16:11	07:29.3	8.0	easy 1:35/1:41				NXT2
8	2/17	Bike	74.00	4:00:00	03:14.6	18.5	good first hour, then fell off fast	140	175	x	CT
8	2/18	Run	1.50	0:15:00	10:00.0	6.0	brick run				TM
8	2/18	Swim	1.85	1:01:21	33:13.4	1.8	recovery swim			xa	5S
8	2/19	Swim	0.94	0:30:39	32:41.6	1.8	tired			xa	5S
8	2/20	Swim	1.79	1:00:39	33:53.2	1.8	tired			s	5S
8	2/21	Bike	16.50	0:51:00	03:05.5	19.4	10-8-6-4-2-1 session 1.2-1.3 RI 3'			xa	CT
8	2/22						rest				
8	2/23	Run	10.50	1:19:47	07:35.9	7.9	JP, JM for half				NXT2
8	2/23	Swim	0.88	0:30:00	34:03.9	1.8	free form, no tracking			xa	5S
9	2/24	Bike	17.00	0:47:46	02:48.6	21.4	disc wheel test, 20mph gusts				SR
9	2/24	Run	6.30	0:43:26	06:53.7	8.7	brick run			a	NXT2
9	3/2	Swim	2.40	1:09:42	29:02.5	2.1	IMNZ02				
9	3/2	Bike	112.00	5:46:50	03:05.8	19.4	IMNZ02				SR
9	3/2	Run	26.20	3:39:18	08:22.2	7.2	IMNZ02				NXT2
10	3/4	Swim	0.45	0:15:07	33:15.4	1.8	recovery			xa	5S
10	3/5	Swim	0.85	0:28:45	33:44.0	1.8	recovery			xas	5S
10	3/7	Swim	0.60	0:19:55	33:11.7	1.8	recovery			xa	5S
10	3/8	Bike	10.00	0:30:00	03:00.0	20.0	CT spin		130	a	CT
10	3/8	Swim	0.88	0:30:00	34:03.9	1.8	recovery			xa	5S
10	3/8	Run	4.60	0:32:05	06:58.5	8.6	NT				NXT2
10	3/9	Run	8.80	1:08:15	07:45.3	7.7	wind warnings			a	NXT2
11	3/10	Run	8.90	1:07:59	07:38.3	7.9	BG+ strong wind			a	NXT2
11	3/11	Run	9.10	1:03:41	06:59.9	8.6	BT loop			a	NXT2
11	3/12	Bike	18.10	1:00:00	03:18.9	18.1	IMUSA	148	186	a	CT
11	3/13	Swim	0.97	0:32:49	33:58.5	1.8	easy			xa	5S
11	3/14									a	
11	3/15	Swim	0.97	0:32:00	33:07.8	1.8	better			xa	5S
11	3/16	Run	9.10	1:02:28	06:51.9	8.7	BT mixed effort			a	NXT2
12	3/17	Run	13.10	1:24:12	06:25.6	9.3	March Madness 1/2 Marathon				NXT2
12	3/18	Swim	1.88	1:02:02	33:05.1	1.8	mixed			as	5S
12	3/19	Run	9.60	1:10:50	07:22.7	8.1					NXT2
12	3/20	Run	8.50	1:04:25	07:34.7	7.9					NXT2
12	3/21										
12	3/22										
12	3/23	Run	8.20	1:03:31	07:44.8	7.7	8xCB grounds			xa	NXT2
13	3/24	Run	7.60	0:57:15	07:32.0	8.0	2x CB loop			xa	NXT2
13	3/25	Swim	1.79	1:00:41	33:54.3	1.8				xa	
13	3/26	Swim	1.82	1:00:03	33:01.7	1.8				xa	
13	3/27	Run	7.60	0:54:19	07:08.8	8.4	2x CB loop			xa	NXT2
13	3/27	Swim	0.91	0:30:16	33:17.6	1.8				xa	
13	3/28	Run	5.00	2:00:00	24:00.0	2.5	hiking mountains			xa	NXT2
13	3/29	Run	7.60	0:56:29	07:25.9	8.1	2x CB loop			xa	NXT2
13	3/30	Run	26.20	3:13:53	07:24.0	8.1	easy 1:34/1:39				NXT2
14	3/31	Bike	18.50	1:00:00	03:14.6	18.5	CT flat	130	160	x	CT
14	4/1	Swim	1.25	0:39:43	31:46.4	1.9				xa	5S
14	4/2	Run	4.60	0:34:49	07:34.1	7.9	recovery				NXT2
14	4/2	Swim	0.97	0:30:45	31:50.1	1.9				xa	5S
14	4/3	Run	9.10	1:03:30	06:58.7	8.6	BT loop			a	NXT2
14	4/3	Bike	10.00	0:35:13	03:31.3	17.0	10 mile intermediate hills CT	156	226	a	CT
14	4/4	Run	6.90	0:49:30	07:10.4	8.4	hybrid			xa	NXT2
14	4/4	Bike	20.00	0:57:17	02:51.9	20.9	3x6x1.5' 30" RI	145	216	a	CT
14	4/5	Run	4.60	0:33:20	07:14.8	8.3	NT loop			a	NXT2
14	4/5	Swim	0.97	0:31:05	32:10.8	1.9				xa	5S
14	4/6	Run	26.20	3:14:15	07:24.8	8.1	hmx2 1:32/1:42			a	NXT2
15	4/7	Run	8.70	0:59:34	06:50.8	8.8	BG loop rain, wind 38d			xa	BT2
15	4/8	Swim	0.97	0:31:18	32:24.3	1.9				xa	5S
15	4/8	Bike	20.00	0:59:00	02:57.0	20.3	20 mi flat	137	197		CT
15	4/9	Run	9.10	1:03:33	06:59.0	8.6	BT				NXT2
15	4/9	Swim	0.97	0:30:29	31:33.6	1.9	w/Rob			xa	5S
15	4/10	Run	6.10	0:43:57	07:12.3	8.3	AU				BT
15	4/10	Swim	0.94	0:30:17	32:18.1	1.9	AU			xa	
15	4/11	Run	9.10	1:00:15	06:37.3	9.1	BT				NXT2
15	4/12						rest			a	

Week	Date	Type	Dist	Time	Pace	MPH	Exercise	HR	Watts	Wts	Shoes
15	4/13	Run	8.70	0:59:56	06:53.3	8.7	easy; ITB			xa	NXT2
16	4/14						travel to Boston				
16	4/15	Run	26.20	2:54:37	06:39.9	9.0	Boston Marathon				NXT2
16	4/16	Swim	0.91	31:15.7	34:23.3	1.7	recovery			xa	5S
16	4/17	Swim	1.05	34:46.8	33:05.3	1.8	recovery			xas	5S
16	4/18	Swim	0.94	0:30:45	32:48.0	1.8	recovery			xa	5S
16	4/18	Bike	20.40	1:00:00	02:56.5	20.4	CT spin	138	199		CT
16	4/19	Run	9.10	0:59:50	06:34.5	9.1	BT				NXG
16	4/20	Bike	30.75	1:53:00	03:40.5	16.3	easy; wind			xa	SR
17	4/21	Bike	36.20	2:00:00	03:18.9	18.1	IMLP CT	140	186	a	CT
17	4/22	Swim	1.02	0:32:23	31:39.8	1.9				xa	5S
17	4/23	Swim	0.88	0:29:53	33:55.9	1.8	10x100 on 2			xa	5S
17	4/23	Bike	20.00	1:00:00	03:00.0	20.0	CT spin	140	194		CT
17	4/24									xa	
17	4/25	Bike	20.10	1:00:00	02:59.1	20.1	CT NZ	145	198		CT
17	4/26	Swim	0.94	0:30:15	32:16.0	1.9				xa	5S
17	4/27	Bike	39.04	2:10:00	03:19.8	18.0	cool, windy, bonk				SR
18	4/28	Run	9.15	1:00:08	06:34.3	9.1	BG+	162		a	NXG
18	4/29	Swim	1.05	0:32:24	30:49.4	1.9	great			xa	5S
18	4/30	Run	9.10	1:02:54	06:54.7	8.7	BT am				NXG
18	4/30	Swim	0.99	0:31:30	31:40.8	1.9				xa	5S
18	5/1	Bike	10.00	0:37:22	03:44.2	16.1	10 mile intermediate hills CT	150	205		CT
18	5/1	Swim	0.97	0:31:13	32:19.1	1.9				xas	5S
18	5/2	Run	5.27	1:00:00	11:23.1	5.3	P1L8 treadmill	154		a	TM
18	5/3	Run	9.35	1:08:26	07:19.1	8.2	BT+			xa	NXG
18	5/4	Bike	46.80	2:31:00	03:13.6	18.6				a	SR
19	5/5	Bike	20.41	1:08:54	03:22.5	17.8				a	SR
19	5/6	Swim	0.97	0:30:54	31:59.4	1.9				xa	5S
19	5/7	Run	9.10	1:03:37	06:59.5	8.6	BT am	156			NXG
19	5/7	Swim	1.45	0:45:24	31:20.1	1.9				xa	5S
19	5/8	Bike	10.00	0:38:30	03:51.0	15.6	10 mile intermediate hills CT	145		a	CT
19	5/8	Swim	1.90	1:00:05	31:34.0	1.9				x	5S
19	5/9	Run	9.10	1:01:59	06:48.7	8.8	BT			a	NXG
19	5/10	Bike	24.00	1:15:00	03:07.5	19.2	3x6x1.5' CT 60'; 6x Tower hill	155		a	CT
19	5/11	Run	26.20	3:10:21	07:15.9	8.3	2xHM	156			NXG
20	5/13	Bike	10.00	0:37:32	03:45.2	16.0	10 mile intermediate hills CT	150		a	CT
20	5/13	Swim	0.99	0:30:36	30:46.5	1.9	sore ribs			xa	5S
20	5/14	Run	3.95	0:45:00	11:23.5	5.3	P1L8 treadmill	145		a	TM
20	5/14	Swim	1.82	1:00:15	33:08.3	1.8	sore ribs			xa	5S
20	5/15	Bike	101.70	5:10:30	03:03.2	19.7	43m; flat; 58.7m			a	SR
20	5/16	Swim	1.82	1:00:15	33:08.3	1.8	sore ribs			xa	5S
20	5/17	Run	9.10	1:08:13	07:29.8	8.0					NXG
20	5/17	Swim	0.94	0:30:54	32:57.6	1.8	sore ribs			xa	5S
20	5/18	Run	13.10	1:40:00	07:38.0	7.9	rough				NXG
21	5/19	Run	9.10	1:02:37	06:52.9	8.7	BT	159		a	NXG
21	5/22	Run	9.10	1:04:41	07:06.5	8.4				a	NXG
21	5/22	Swim	0.97	0:31:54	33:01.6	1.8	sore ribs			xa	5S
21	5/23	Bike	20.00	0:59:57	02:59.9	20.0	20 mi flat	146	196	a	CT
21	5/24	Run	9.10	0:57:02	06:16.0	9.6	BT			a	NXG
21	5/25	Bike	20.00	0:59:08	02:57.4	20.3	20 mi flat	144	202	a	CT
22	5/26	Run	26.20	2:59:12	06:50.4	8.8	MadCity Marathon				NXG
22	5/27	Run	3.14	0:28:24	09:02.7	6.6	Jubilee Jog 5k with Amanda				NXG
22	5/28	Bike	6.00	0:20:00	03:20.0	18.0	easy spin				CT
22	5/28	Swim	0.65	0:20:09	30:50.3	1.9	AU drills/paddles			xa	
22	5/29	Swim	0.59	0:18:51	31:44.8	1.9					5S
22	5/30	Run	56.00	2:47:20	02:59.3	20.1	IMNZ lap 1	158	208		CT
22	5/31	Swim	1.00	0:30:35	30:35.0	2.0				xas	5S
22	6/1	Bike	37.25	1:53:30	03:02.8	19.7	GL+			xa	SR
23	6/2	Bike	40.25	2:04:30	03:05.6	19.4	wu some 23 intervals			xa	SR
23	6/3	Bike	23.94	1:14:36	03:07.0	19.3	LF				SR
23	6/3	Swim	0.99	0:31:07	31:17.7	1.9				x	5S
23	6/4	Bike	10.00	0:35:20	03:32.0	17.0	10 mile intermediate hills CT	156	223		CT
23	6/4	Run	2.40	0:25:00	10:25.0	5.8	P1L8 treadmill	156			TM
23	6/4	Swim	1.96	1:01:09	31:11.7	1.9				xa	5S
23	6/5	Swim	0.99	0:29:59	30:09.3	2.0				xa	5S
23	6/6	Run	9.10	1:02:42	06:53.4	8.7	BT			a	NXG
23	6/6	Swim	1.03	0:30:06	29:11.3	2.1	25m pool			s	5S
23	6/7	Bike	23.95	1:11:20	02:58.7	20.1	LF				SR
23	6/7	Swim	1.53	0:46:52	30:36.4	2.0	25m pool			xa	5S
23	6/8	Bike	50.28	2:32:17	03:01.7	19.8					SR
24	6/9	Run	13.10	1:22:54	06:19.7	9.5	North Shore 1/2 Marathon			a	NXG

Week	Date	Type	Dist	Time	Pace	MPH	Exercise	HR	Watts	Wts	Shoes
24	6/10						travel/rest			xa	
24	6/11	Bike	26.90	1:20:00	02:58 4	20.2	LF+V				SR
24	6/11	Swim	1.94	1:01:05	31:31.6	1.9	outside			xa	5S
24	6/12	Bike	28.08	1:24:54	03:01.4	19.8	LF+V			xa	SR
24	6/13	Run	9.40	1:06:56	07.07.2	8.4	BT+				NXG
24	6/14	Bike	26.88	1:17:22	02:52.7	20.8	LF+V				SR
24	6/14	Swim	1.39	0:43:30	31:14.9	1.9	35@.30 45+ 15@12:45 6/12			xa	5S
24	6/15	Bike	50.25	2:30:42	02:59.9	20.0					SR
25	6/16	Run	13.10	1:29:59	06:52.1	8.7	HM				NXG
25	6/18	Run	8.10	1:00:00	07:24.4	8.1	Rochester			xa	NXG1
25	6/19	Run	7.20	0:54:30	07:34.2	7.9	Rochester			xa	NXG1
25	6/20	Bike	26.88	1:16:30	02:50.8	21.1	LF+V	150		a	SR
25	6/21	Bike	26.90	1:16:54	02:51 5	21.0	LF+V	153			SR
25	6/21	Swim	0.66	0:20:29	31:12.8	1.9				xa	5S
25	6/22	Bike	107.60	5:24:00	03:00.7	19.9	Hebron	146			SR
26	6/23	Run	8.70	0:58:35	06:44.0	8.9	BG	162			NXG1
26	6/24	Bike	26.89	1:19:42	02:57.8	20.2	LF+V			a	SR
26	6/24	Swim	1.94	1:00:42	31:19.7	1.9	outside			xa	5S
26	6/25	Bike	16.99	1:08:42	04:02 6	14.8	wu 10x(Tower+Lloyd hills) wd			a	SR
26	6/26	Run	5.27	1:00:00	11:23.1	5.3	P1L8 treadmill				TM
26	6/26	Swim	0.94	0:30:03	32:03.2	1.9	easy outside				5S
26	6/27	Bike	26.90	1:18:16	02:54 6	20.6	LF+V	147			SR
26	6/27	Swim	1.19	0:36:54	31:04.4	1.9	outside			xa	5S
26	6/28	Swim	1.00	0:30:29	30:29.0	2.0	outside			xa	5S
26	6/29	Run	26.20	3:02:59	06:59 0	8.6	first 1 32 10; second 1 30 49				NXG
27	6/30	Bike	32.12	1:37:12	03:01.6	19.8	WTB				SR
27	7/1	Bike	26.90	1:16:22	02:50 3	21.1	LF+V				SR
27	7/1	Swim	1.41	0:43:44	31:06.0	1.9				xa	5S
27	7/3	Bike	14.97	0:59:49	03:59.7	15.0	Vwu+10xT+10xL+Vwd				SR
27	7/3	Run	9.55	1:06:41	06:59.0	8.6	BT+				NXG1
27	7/4	Bike	26.90	1:14:34	02:46 3	21.6	LF+V				SR
27	7/4	Run	3.10	0:18:50	06:04.5	9.9	Winnetka 5k brick				NXG1
27	7/5	Bike	101.54	4:59:20	02:56.9	20.4	44+33+24 loops			xa	SR
27	7/6	Run	13.10	1:31:33	06:59.3	8.6	HM	155		xa	NXG
28	7/7	Bike	31.00	1:33:00	03:00.0	20.0	WTB				SR
28	7/8	Bike	27.10	1:19:57	02:57 0	20.3	LFFS+	148		a	SR
28	7/9	Run	9.10	1:04:07	07:02.7	8.5	BT	148		a	NXG1
28	7/9	Swim	1.88	1:00:36	32:19.2	1.9	outside			x	5S
28	7/10	Bike	9.12	0:47:10	05:10.3	11.6	10xTower+10xLloyd hills to L2			a	SR
28	7/10	Swim	1.91	1:00:20	31:39.0	1.9				a	5S
28	7/11	Bike	26.60	1:17:30	02:54.8	20.6	LF+V				SR
28	7/11	Run	2.20	0:14:37	06:38 6	9.0	brick				NXG1
28	7/12	Swim	1 03	0:31:57	30:58.9	1.9				xa	5S
28	7/13	Bike	37.93	1:49:00	02:52.4	20.9	brick part 1				SR
28	7/13	Run	13.10	1:30:22	06:53 9	8.7	HM loop brick/ felt on run				NXG1
29	7/14	Run	13.10	1:39:02	07:33.6	7.9	sore shoulder recovery run	150		a	NXG1
29	7/15	Bike	10.25	0:30:15	02:57.1	20.3					SR
29	7/15	Swim	0.66	0:20:37	31:25.0	1.9	sore shoulder; recovery			x	5S
29	7/16	Run	4.30	0:31:36	07:20.9	8.2	ATL			xa	NXG1
29	7/17	Bike	8.86	0:34:51	03:56.0	15.3	wu 10xTower up to 12mph			a	SR
29	7/18	Bike	26.80	1:12:38	02:42.6	22.1	Zipps TT				SR
29	7/18	Swim	0.66	0:20:25	31:06.7	1.9					5S
29	7/19	Bike	21.74	1:01:40	02:50.2	21.2	2xGW loop	152		xa	SR
29	7/20	Run	9.10	1:04:30	07:05.3	8.5	sore ribs			a	NXG
30	7/21	Bike	38.00	1:44:00	02:44.2	21.9	brick part 1 Zipp	156			SR
30	7/21	Run	2.20	0:14:59	06:48 6	8.8	brick part 2	156		a	NXG1
30	7/22	Bike	9.90	0:29:40	02:59.8	20.0	spin			a	SR
30	7/23	Run	6.90	0:50:47	07:21.6	8.2	easy				NXG1
30	7/24	Bike	9.90	0:32:10	03:14.9	18.5	nothing				SR
30	7/24	Swim	0.66	0:20:47	31:40.2	1.9	sore shoulder			xa	5S
30	7/26	Swim	0.30	0:12:00	40:00.0	1.5					
30	7/26	Bike	12.40	0:42:00	03:23 2	17.7	LP			a	SR
30	7/27	Swim	0.30	0:12:00	40:00.0	1.5					
30	7/27	Bike	8.00	0:24:00	03:00.0	20.0				a	SR
31	7/28	Swim	2.40	1.10:41	29:27 1	2.0	Ironman USA Lake Placid				
31	7/28	Bike	112.00	5:41:07	03:02.7	19.7	Ironman USA Lake Placid				SR
31	7/28	Run	26.20	3:33:50	08:09.7	7.4	Ironman USA Lake Placid				NXG1
31	7/31	Bike	20.40	1:00:23	02:57 6	20.3	2xGW loop				SR
31	8/1	Bike	21.80	1:05:51	03:01.2	19.9	FS+V				SR

Week	Date	Type	Dist	Time	Pace	MPH	Exercise	HR	Watts	Wts	Shoes
31	8/1	Swim	0.66	0:20:39	31:28.0	1.9	recovery			a	5S
31	8/2	Run	8.60	1:00:35	07:02.7	8.5	recovery	160		xa	NXG
31	8/3	Bike	39.70	1:54:49	02:53.5	20.7	WTB+David	160		xa	SR
32	8/4	Bike	35.30	1:56:44	03:18.4	18.1	w/David	154		a	SR
32	8/4	Swim	0.43	0:15:00	35:12.0	1.7	taping; intervals				5S
32	8/5	Run	4.60	0:32:55	07:09.3	8.4	recovery	154		a	NXG
32	8/5	Swim	0.80	0:25:00	31:25.7	1.9	wu/drills			xa	5S
32	8/6	Swim	0.91	0:30:46	33:50.6	1.8	wu/drills/wd			xa	5S
32	8/7	Bike	14.30	1:01:30	04:18.0	14.0	mixed hill/strength repeats			a	SR
32	8/7	Swim	0.91	0:30:11	33:12.1	1.8	15x50 ~ 46-47 on 60			a	5S
32	8/8	Swim	0.94	0:30:03	32:03.2	1.9	form			a	5S
32	8/9	Run	12.10	1:21:06	06:42.1	9.0	w/BH				NXG1
32	8/10	Bike	37.10	1:55:13	03:06.3	19.3	WTB long wu			a	SR
33	8/11	Run	18.40	2:03:41	06:43.3	8.9	18.2@2:03:41 + 0:01:19	158		a	NXG
33	8/12	Bike	21.80	1:05:11	02:59.4	20.1	FS+V	150			SR
33	8/13	Swim	0.94	0:30:23	32:24.5	1.9	wu/drills/wd			xa	5S
33	8/14	Run	4.60	0:32:30	07:03.9	8.5	NT recoovery	152			NXG
33	8/14	Swim	1.05	0:32:55	31:18.9	1.9				xa	5S
33	8/15	Bike	26.70	1:15:20	02:49.3	21.3	LF+V				SR
33	8/15	Swim	0.97	0:30:07	31:05.3	1.9	outside			xa	5S
33	8/16	Bike	26.70	1:16:11	02:51.2	21.0	LF+V			a	SR
33	8/17	Run	26.20	3:09:51	07:14.8	8.3	HMX2 1:33/1:36	155		a	NXG
34	8/18	Bike	45.10	2:30:00	03:19.6	18.0	Barrington				SR
34	8/19	Swim	0.91	30:04.4	33:04.8	1.8	wu/drills/wd			xa	5S
34	8/20	Run	8.50	1:07:09	07:54.0	7.6	Glencoe+5xTower Hill	156		a	NXG1
34	8/20	Swim	1.05	0:32:18	30:43.7	2.0	time trial			xa	5S
34	8/21	Bike	21.80	1:01:34	02:49.4	21.2	FS+V			xa	SR
34	8/22	Bike	10.00	0:36:11	03:37.1	16.6	10 mile intermediate hills CT	153	210		CT
34	8/22	Run	1.60	0:15:00	09:22.5	6.4	TM brick	158	1%		TM
34	8/22	Swim	0.99	0:31:03	31:13.6	1.9				xa	5S
34	8/23	Run	9.70	1:08:04	07:01.0	8.6	wu/tempo	147/163			NXG
34	8/23	Swim	0.94	0:30:11	32:11.7	1.9	brick/recovery				5S
34	8/25	Swim	0.94	0:26:45	28:32.0	2.1	Mrs. T's				
34	8/25	Bike	24.80	1:01:15	02:28.2	24.3	Mrs. T's				SR
34	8/25	Run	6.20	0:39:53	06:26.0	9.3	Mrs. T's				NXG1
35	8/26	Swim	1.06	34:06.3	32:05.9	1.9	recovery			xa	5S
35	8/28	Run	5.40	0:41:58	07:46.3	7.7	Boston run			xa	
35	8/30	Run	3.70	0:28:22	07:40.0	7.8	Nantucket			xa	
35	8/31	Run	4.80	0:36:48	07:40.0	7.8	Nantucket			a	
36	9/1	Run	4.10	0:31:44	07:44.4	7.8	Nantucket			a	
36	9/2	Run	4.50	0:34:58	07:46.2	7.7	Nantucket			a	
36	9/4	Bike	10.00	0:38:50	03:53.0	15.5	10 mile intermediate hills CT	164	179		CT
36	9/4	Swim	0.91	0:30:30	33:33.0	1.8	TI drills			xa	5S
36	9/5	Bike	20.00	1:00:00	03:00.0	20.0	Kona first 20	L3	214		CT
36	9/5	Swim	0.94	0:30:30	32:32.0	1.8	easy TI			xa	5S
36	9/6	Swim	1.05	0:33:12	31:35.1	1.9	TI			xn	5S
36	9/7	Bike	39.00	2:00:55	03:06.0	19.4	WTB			a	SR
37	9/8	Run	13.10	1:26:09	06:34.6	9.1	HM loop			xa	NXG1
37	9/9	Bike	15.40	0:46:17	03:00.3	20.0	spin			a	SR
37	9/9	Swim	0.63	0:19:53	31:48.8	1.9	easy				CT
37	9/10	Run	8.50	1:01:53	07:16.8	8.2	easy				NXG1
37	9/11	Bike	11.80	0:34:03	02:53.1	20.8					SR
37	9/12	Swim	0.65	0:20:00	30:36.5	2.0	drills			xan	5S
37	9/13	Bike	5.70	0:20:00	03:30.5	17.1	test				SR
38	9/15	Swim	2.40	1:15:29	31:27.1	1.9	Ironman Wisconsin				
38	9/15	Bike	112.00	5:37:58	03:01.1	19.9	Ironman Wisconsin				SR
38	9/15	Run	26.20	3:36:16	08:15.3	7.3	Ironman Wisconsin				NXG1
38	9/17	Swim	0.45	0:15:04	33:08.8	1.8	recovery			xa	5S
38	9/18	Swim	0.48	0:15:29	32:03.6	1.9	recovery			xa	5S
38	9/20	Swim	0.68	0:21:37	31:42.3	1.9	recovery			xa	5S
38	9/21	Bike	30.60	1:36:17	03:08.8	19.1	WTB			xa	SR
39	9/22	Run	6.30	0:47:29	07:32.2	8.0	recovery			xa	NXG1
39	9/23	Bike	19.25	1:00:30	03:08.6	19.1	Kona first 20	150	214		CT
39	9/24	Swim	1.05	0:33:27	31:49.4	1.9				xa	5S
39	9/25	Bike	25.00	1:10:48	02:49.9	21.2	3x6x2.8x260watts RI 30" 10'w/u	L3	232	a	CT
39	9/26	Swim	1.88	1:00:03	32:01.6	1.9				a	5S

Week	Date	Type	Dist	Time	Pace	MPH	Exercise	HR	Watts	Wts	Shoes
39	9/27	Run	9.10	1:06:19	07.17.3	8.2	BT			a	NXG1
39	9/28	Run	10.90	1:21:57	07:31.1	8.0	JP hill route			a	NXG1
40	9/29	Bike	29.10	1:30:00	03:05.6	19.4	Kona first 29	150	205	a	CT
40	9/30	Swim	0.48	0:15:10	31:24.2	1.9				xa	5S
40	9/30	Bike	18.20	1:00:00	03:17.8	18.2	Kona first 18	150	181	a	CT
40	10/1	Bike	27.20	1:46:23	03:54.7	15.3	Kona 30 to Hawi withdwind	150	193		CT
40	10/1	Run	1.60	0:15:00	09.22.5	6.4	brick after CT	150	1%	a	TM
40	10/2	Bike	13.00	0:42:32	03:16.3	18.3	10'wu + PR 10milint 32.32	168	257	a	CT
40	10/2	Run	2.80	0:24:00	08:34.3	7.0	brick after CT	160	1%	xa	TM
40	10/3	Run	8.60	1:00:33	07:02.4	8.5	LT			a	NXG
40	10/5	Bike	27.00	1:28:00	03:15.6	18.4	WTB			a	SR
41	10/6	Run	6.20	0:39:01	06:17.6	9.5	Winnetka 10k			a	NXG1
41	10/9	Swim	1.88	1:01:20	32:42.7	1.8				xa	5S
41	10/9	Run	9.10	0:57:15	06:17.5	9.5	BT				NXG2
41	10/10	Bike	60.30	3:01:48	03:00.9	19.9	(GL+V) + (LF+V)				SR
41	10/12	Run	3.50	0:26:22	07:32.0	8.0	easy				NXG
42	10/13	Run	26.20	3:05:32	07:04.9	8.5	Chicago Marathon				NXG1
42	10/14	Swim	0.45	0:14:44	32:24.8	1.9	recovery			xa	5S
42	10/19	Swim	2.40	1:18:57	32:53.8	1.8	Ironman Hawaii				5S
42	10/19	Bike	112.00	6:01:54	03:13.9	18.6	Ironman Hawaii				SR
42	10/19	Run	26.20	3:50:14	08:47.3	6.8	Ironman Hawaii				NXG2
43	10/26	Run	6.00	0:45:32	07:35.3	7.9	recovery			xa	NXG2
44	10/27	Bike	9.00	0:30:00	03.20.0	18.0	CT spin		140	xa	CT
44	10/29	Swim	0.82	0:25:46	31:16.5	1.9	recovery			xa	5S
44	10/30	Swim	0.80	0:25:36	32:11.0	1.9	recovery			xa	5S
44	11/2	Run	3.60	0:27:08	07:32.2	8.0	recovery			xa	NXG2
45	11/4	Swim	0.91	0:28:47	31:39.7	1.9	recovery			xa	5S
45	11/8	Swim	0.91	0:28:53	31:46.3	1.9	recovery			x	5S
45	11/9	Run	8.50	1:06:01	07:46.0	7.7	Jog/walk with Eric/Kirsten			xa	NXG2
46	11/10	Run	8.70	1:02:16	07:09.4	8.4	pushing Kirsten in baby jogger			a	NXG2
46	11/12	Bike	10.00	0:36:25	03:38.5	16.5	10 mile intermediate hills CT	L2	210	xa	CT
46	11/12	Run	2.00	0:24:00	12:00.0	5.0	P1L7 hill TM brick	158		xa	TM
46	11/13	Bike	20.00	0:56:11	02:48.6	21.4	Twenty mile flat CT 95 cadence	Z2 Z3	227	xa	CT
46	11/14	Run	5.27	1:00:00	11:23.1	5.3	P1L8 treadmill hills	Run Z1		xa	TM
46	11/16	Run	8.60	1:05:32	07:37.2	7.9				a	NXG1
47	11/18	Bike	20.00	0:58:36	02:55.8	20.5	Twenty mile flat CT 90 cadence	Z3-L1	210	xa	CT
47	11/19	Swim	0.94	0:29:44	31:42.9	1.9				xa	5S
47	11/20	Run	9.10	1:00:46	06:40.7	9.0	BT			xa	NXG2
47	11/21	Bike	25.00	1:10:00	02:48.0	21.4	Twenty-five mile flat 95-95	L1-L3	230	a	CT
48	11/24	Bike	25.00	1:10:00	02:48.0	21.4	Twenty-five mile flat 90-95	L2-L3	230	xa	CT
48	11/25	Run	3.50	0:31:00	08:51.4	6.8	TM various	144		xa	TM
48	11/26	Bike	21.80	1:05:00	02:58.9	20.1	CT IMNZ various	Z3-L1	220	xa	CT
48	11/27	Run	8.60	1:06:44	07:45.6	7.7	easy run in snow			xa	NXG2
48	11/28	Run	8.60	1:04:05	07:27.1	8.1	NL Loop; 20 degrees			xa	NXG2
48	11/29	Run	6.20	0:47:24	07:38.7	7.8				xa	NXG2
48	11/30	Run	13.40	1:44:29	07:47.8	7.7	HM+beach+; cold, windy			xa	NXG2
49	12/1	Bike	22.00	1:04:20	02:55.5	20.5	CT flat	Z2-Z3	213	xa	CT
49	12/2	Run	5.75	1:00:00	10:26.1	5.8	TM 45' P1L7 + 15' 1% 7.7	Run 2 6%-10		xa	TM
49	12/4	Bike	19.00	1:00:00	03.09.5	19.0	10' wu + 50' Kona CT	Z3	213	xa	CT
49	12/5	Swim	0.88	0:28:42	32:35.3	1.8					5S
49	12/6	Swim	0.94	0:29:18	31:15.2	1.9	better			xa	5S
49	12/7	Run	7.80	0:56:57	07:18.1	8.2	SG Gillson				NXG1
50	12/8	Bike	16.80	1:00:00	03:34.3	16.8	CDTO CT course	Z3-L1	209	a	CT
50	12/9	Run	5.27	1:00:00	11:23.1	5.3	P1L8 TM hill course	Run Z2		a	TM
50	12/10	Bike	15.00	0:50:30	03:22.0	17.8	15 mile intervals inter/intermed CT	Z3-L3	230	a	CT
50	12/11	Swim	1.85	1:00:35	32:48.5	1.8	easy			x	5S
50	12/12	Swim	1.88	1:00:34	32:18.1	1.9				x	5S
50	12/13	Run	6.20	0:47:41	07:41.5	7.8	LT am			a	NXG3
50	12/14	Run	12.50	1:29:28	07:09.4	8.4	BSL 6&7; 3 in ice; late hills			a	NXG3
51	12/15	Run	10.00	1:15:58	07:35.8	7.9	BH+ to/from HP			a	NXG3
51	12/16	Bike	20.00	1:00:30	03.01.5	19.8	spin	Z1-Z2			CT
51	12/18	Bike	21.44	1:00:00	02:47.9	21.4	3x6x1.5' RI 30" 2'RI	L1-L3	230	a	CT
51	12/19	Run	3.90	0:25:30	06:32.3	9.2	crash at Gillson				NXG3
52	12/25	Bike	20.20	1:00:00	02:58.2	20.2	CT flat recovery ride	Z3-L1	205	xa	CT
52	12/26	Run	9.10	1:11:22	07:53.5	7.6	BT half snow/recovery	easy		a	NXG1
52	12/27	Run	9.10	1:11:29	07:51.3	7.6	BT 15 degrees; snow; bonk	170+		a	NXG
52	12/27	Bike	26.20	1:15:00	02:51.8	21.0	IMNZ 26.2 of lap 1	L1-L3	223	a	CT
52	12/28	Run	9.10	1:05:30	07.11.9	8.3	BT loop -- better!	165ish			NXG2
52	12/28	Bike	28.00	1:18:49	02:48.9	21.3	IMNZ 28 of lap 1	L1-L2	225	a	CT
53	12/29	Run	9.10	1:03:50	07:00.9	8.6	BT	165			NXG2
53	12/30	Run	13.10	1:31:23	06:58.5	8.6	HM	162			NXG2
53	12/31	Run	13.10	1:33:57	07:10.3	8.4	HM sore knee	162			NXG2

2002 Breakdown of Time, Location and Equipment

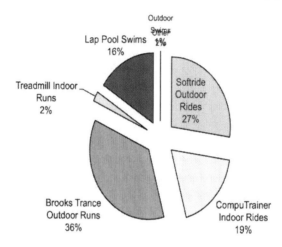

2002 Equipment

Shoes	Data	Total	Pace/mile
5S	Sum of Time	68:35:04	
	Sum of Dist	127.7	0:32:14
	Count of Dist	107.0	
BT	Sum of Time	0:43:57	
	Sum of Dist	6.1	0:07:12
	Count of Dist	1.0	
BT2	Sum of Time	0:59:34	
	Sum of Dist	8.7	0:06:51
	Count of Dist	1.0	
CT	Sum of Time	79:38:10	
	Sum of Dist	1,536.4	0:03:07
	Count of Dist	65.0	
NXG	Sum of Time	40:34:57	
	Sum of Dist	346.3	0:07:02
	Count of Dist	30.0	
NXG1	Sum of Time	33:24:58	
	Sum of Dist	272.6	0:07:21
	Count of Dist	27.0	
NXG2	Sum of Time	19:06:34	
	Sum of Dist	152.4	0:07:31
	Count of Dist	15.0	
NXG3	Sum of Time	3:58:37	
	Sum of Dist	32.6	0:07:19
	Count of Dist	4.0	
NXT	Sum of Time	6:28:15	
	Sum of Dist	54.3	0:07:09
	Count of Dist	5.0	
NXT2	Sum of Time	50:03:32	
	Sum of Dist	397.0	0:07:34
	Count of Dist	36.0	
SR	Sum of Time	117:28:43	
	Sum of Dist	2,295.0	0:03:04
	Count of Dist	65.0	
TM	Sum of Time	9:41:12	
	Sum of Dist	55.2	0:10:32
	Count of Dist	16.0	
(blank)	Sum of Time	12:26:12	
	Sum of Dist	40.5	
	Count of Dist	18.0	
Total Sum of Time		443:09:45	
Total Sum of Dist		5,324.8	
Total Count of Dist		390.0	

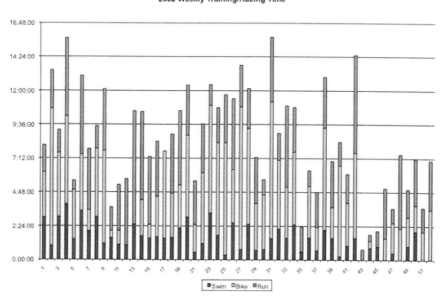

2002 Weekly Training/Racing Time

Swim, Bike, Run

	1994	1995	1996	1997	1998	1999	2000	2001	2002
Miles	150.0	1,553.4	2,594.1	3,056.5	3,803.3	3,502.2	2,928.4	4,089.2	5,324.8
Time	21:52:30	193:35:54	287:54:32	307:08:21	316:21:30	309:20:43	279:34:49	375:33:07	443:09:45
Sessions				282	289	261	259	366	390
Distance/Session				10.8	13.2	13.4	11.3	11.2	13.65
Time/session				1:05:21	1:05:41	1:11.07	1:04:46	1:01:34	1:08:11
Time/mile	08:45	07.29	06:40	06:02	04:59	05:18	05:44	05:31	04:59.6
Time/week	1:12:55	3:43:23	5:32:12	5:54:23	6:05.02	5:56:56	5:22:36	7:12:09	8:31:20

Run

	1994	1995	1996	1997	1998	1999	2000	2001	2002
Miles	150.0	1,251.1	1,624.8	1,206.0	1,097.2	1,198.7	1,387.3	1,522.1	1,347.7
Time	21:52:30	168:33:04	205:10:19	165:48:34	147:12:06	175:21:31	184:41:38	187:16:16	167:55:26
Sessions				145	133	134	176	163	140
Distance/Session				8.3	8.2	8.9	7.9	9.3	9.63
Time/session				1:08:37	1:06:24	1:18:31	1:02:58	1:08:56	1:11:58
Time/mile	08:45	08:05	07:35	08:15	0.08:03	0.08:47	0:07:59	0:07:23	07:28.6

Bike

	1994	1995	1996	1997	1998	1999	2000	2001	2002
Miles	-	290.0	925.7	1,781.5	2,667.9	2,276.1	1,525.8	2,463.6	3,830.8
Time	0:00:00	17:24:14	55:33:16	101:38:28	147:32:39	119:14:11	85:49:19	130:40:23	196:47:00
Sessions				78	120	101	70	107	129
Distance/Session				22.8	22.2	22.5	21.8	23.0	29.70
Time/session				1:18:11	1:13:46	1:10:50	1:13:34	1:13:16	1:31:32
Time/mile	00:00	03:36	03:36	03:25	03:19	03:09	03:22	03:11	03:04.9

Swim

	1994	1995	1996	1997	1998	1999	2000	2001	2002
Miles	-	12.3	43.6	68.9	38.2	27.4	15.3	103.5	146.3
Time	0:00:00	7:38:37	27:10:57	39.41:19	21:36.45	14:45:01	9:03:52	57:36:28	78:27:19
Sessions				59	36	26	13	96	121
Distance/Session				1.2	1.1	1.1	1.2	1.1	1.21
Time/session				0:40:22	0:36:01	0:34:02	0:41:50	0:36:00	0:38:54
Time/mile	00:00	37:24	37:24	34:32	0:33:57	0:32:17	0:35:32	0:33:24	32:10.2

Appendix 2:

Sample Kona Qualifying Times:

By Race, Division

Ironman Arizona 2008 Qualifying Times

Division	Swim	T1	Bike	T2	Run	Total
M18-24	1:03:56	4:16	4:55:16	2:38	3:24:17	9:30:22
M25-29	52:37:00	4:24	4:44:44	1:55	3:08:57	8:52:36
M25-29	55:31:00	4:19	4:59:55	1:33	3:11:29	9:12:45
M25-29	57:41:00	4:41	4:48:50	2:22	3:24:22	9:17:54
M30-34	50:08:00	3:29	4:57:29	2:52	3:14:25	9:08:21
M30-34	56:41:00	3:31	4:56:46	0:59	3:14:04	9:11:58
M30-34	1:01:00	4:01	4:55:02	1:12	3:11:31	9:12:45
M30-34	1:00:57	3:08	5:09:59	1:11	3:13:11	9:28:24
M30-34	56:35:00	4:30	4:59:33	1:54	3:27:16	9:29:46
M30-34	59:38:00	4:11	4:55:47	1:56	3:28:28	9:29:59
M30-34	59:01:00	5:47	5:11:41	3:08	3:14:38	9:34:13
M35-39	1:00:03	4:01	4:57:35	2:36	3:11:16	9:15:28
M35-39	50:23:00	4:45	5:01:30	2:44	3:22:06	9:21:26
M35-39	1:01:12	4:01	5:03:12	2:14	3:11:25	9:22:01
M35-39	1:03:48	4:27	4:58:25	2:25	3:14:01	9:23:05
M35-39	56:55:00	4:15	5:10:36	1:30	3:16:10	9:29:25
M35-39	1:07:07	5:16	5:02:36	3:34	3:12:44	9:31:15
M35-39	1:03:46	4:59	4:55:19	1:41	3:26:04	9:31:47
M35-39	58:35:00	4:42	5:07:16	2:56	3:26:36	9:40:03
M35-39	1:02:34	4:34	5:10:05	1:47	3:21:42	9:40:41
M35-39	1:02:12	4:19	5:05:43	1:37	3:30:38	9:44:27
M40-44	50:24:00	3:30	4:56:06	1:47	3:19:53	9:11:38
M40-44	59:58:00	3:37	4:57:40	2:07	3:20:22	9:23:41
M40-44	1:02:17	4:42	5:02:30	3:23	3:11:51	9:24:39
M40-44	53:42:00	4:49	4:51:25	3:10	3:36:06	9:29:11
M40-44	1:01:57	3:41	4:58:18	2:33	3:32:02	9:38:30
M40-44	51:45:00	4:17	5:10:56	3:37	3:32:48	9:43:21
M40-44	57:02:00	4:49	5:07:39	2:20	3:34:48	9:46:36
M40-44	1:05:17	4:04	5:05:27	1:38	3:32:34	9:48:58
M40-44	1:10:08	4:28	5:03:36	3:20	3:30:37	9:52:07
M40-44	1:04:23	4:23	5:06:30	1:34	3:37:12	9:54:01
M40-44	1:05:05	5:05	4:59:18	2:07	3:42:39	9:54:13
M45-49	56:18:00	5:35	4:59:43	2:58	3:30:52	9:35:24
M45-49	59:35:00	5:34	5:15:41	1:43	3:22:54	9:45:25
M45-49	1:09:32	5:57	5:05:19	1:42	3:25:33	9:48:01
M45-49	1:01:33	3:44	4:56:16	1:46	3:45:52	9:49:09
M45-49	1:11:45	4:47	5:05:22	2:23	3:28:05	9:52:20
M45-49	59:14:00	3:30	5:18:07	2:09	3:30:21	9:53:19
M45-49	1:07:20	6:40	5:06:00	2:36	3:30:57	9:53:32

Ironman Arizona 2008 Qualifying Times						
Division	Swim	T1	Bike	T2	Run	Total
M50-54	1:05:52	4:25	5:06:20	2:10	3:37:10	9:55:56
M50-54	58:31:00	4:03	4:59:06	1:38	4:12:14	10:15:30
M50-54	1:03:00	6:04	5:24:48	2:26	3:39:43	10:16:00
M50-54	1:03:03	4:36	5:01:13	2:17	4:13:54	10:25:01
M50-54	1:08:46	6:28	4:54:10	1:23	4:17:47	10:28:34
M55-59	1:13:27	8:52	5:12:05	1:48	3:54:08	10:30:18
M55-59	1:08:21	5:45	5:31:22	4:51	4:05:12	10:55:29
M60-64	1:23:40	10:35	5:46:38	2:46	4:22:13	11:45:50
M65-69	1:42:50	8:32	5:48:03	6:23	5:11:16	12:57:01
M70-74	1:30:13	13:35	7:22:44	7:18	6:47:19	16:01:06
M75-79	1:38:33	8:17	7:24:24	5:11	6:52:29	16:08:52
MPRO	48:04:00	2:29	4:26:45	1:57	3:00:12	8:19:25
MPRO	52:46:00	2:54	4:30:51	2:18	2:52:46	8:21:34
MPRO	46:15:00	2:37	4:38:07	5:08	2:50:58	8:23:03
MPRO	52:53:00	3:05	4:30:31	1:34	2:56:12	8:24:13
MPRO	50:23:00	2:37	4:46:16	1:12	2:46:53	8:27:20
MPRO	47:58:00	2:40	4:35:59	1:11	3:06:48	8:34:34
W18-24	1:03:48	7:47	5:37:41	3:12	3:39:28	10:31:54
W25-29	55:31:00	4:38	5:26:10	2:35	3:36:53	10:05:45
W25-29	1:12:59	4:54	5:25:03	2:07	3:35:56	10:20:58
W30-34	52:35:00	3:58	5:15:37	2:04	3:42:27	9:56:41
W30-34	1:05:11	5:52	5:34:23	4:04	3:33:52	10:23:20
W30-34	1:08:11	5:03	5:35:42	2:30	3:38:32	10:29:55
W30-34	1:01:52	4:51	5:36:57	1:51	3:49:22	10:34:52
W35-39	1:09:10	5:34	5:19:06	2:48	3:56:30	10:33:06
W35-39	1:07:26	4:57	5:30:23	2:58	3:49:13	10:34:55
W35-39	1:25:53	5:57	5:18:13	2:22	3:51:59	10:44:22
W35-39	1:03:07	5:25	5:34:04	2:45	4:05:03	10:50:22
W40-44	59:59:00	6:18	5:16:20	4:40	3:42:45	10:10:01
W40-44	1:10:04	4:59	5:34:12	1:30	3:39:00	10:29:43
W40-44	1:05:06	5:25	5:43:49	2:34	3:44:08	10:41:01
W40-44	1:08:21	5:12	5:22:08	3:31	4:08:46	10:47:56
W45-49	1:08:11	5:49	5:40:34	3:06	3:51:34	10:49:13
W45-49	1:07:18	4:27	5:36:51	2:02	4:03:42	10:54:18
W45-49	1:11:14	9:32	5:24:35	2:38	4:09:46	10:57:44
W50-54	1:17:35	6:13	5:42:09	2:02	4:12:02	11:20:00
W50-54	1:00:32	6:14	5:56:58	4:32	4:34:59	11:43:14
W55-59	1:12:49	4:27	6:03:00	2:20	5:38:30	13:01:05
W60-64	1:09:01	6:25	6:08:29	4:06	4:40:12	12:08:11
WPRO	1:06:05	2:58	5:02:46	1:23	3:07:56	9:21:06
WPRO	48:13:00	2:40	5:11:23	1:37	3:21:16	9:25:07

Ironman Wisconsin 2008 Qualifying Times					
Division	Swim	T1	Bike	T2	Run	Total
M18-24	1:00:21	5:24	5:04:31	2:28	3:02:29	9:15:12
M18-24	1:02:37	6:04	5:11:28	2:03	3:15:20	9:37:30
M18-24	1:03:16	5:10	5:23:39	1:40	3:13:08	9:46:51
M25-29	1:03:00	5:42	5:10:05	2:01	3:03:55	9:24:41
M25-29	1:09:31	4:56	5:13:32	3:02	3:03:31	9:34:30
M25-29	57:50:00	5:19	5:18:45	3:28	3:13:30	9:38:49
M25-29	59:03:00	5:35	5:15:23	3:47	3:15:46	9:39:32
M30-34	1:02:41	6:11	4:54:38	2:04	3:01:24	9:06:56
M30-34	1:02:03	5:31	5:05:22	2:25	3:17:23	9:32:43
M30-34	1:02:52	6:29	5:02:48	1:43	3:25:23	9:39:13
M30-34	1:02:54	5:52	5:28:59	1:51	3:00:43	9:40:19
M30-34	57:21:00	6:18	5:21:15	1:58	3:20:12	9:47:02
M30-34	57:19:00	6:18	5:21:52	4:17	3:18:14	9:47:59
M30-34	53:20:00	5:08	5:21:48	3:32	3:28:12	9:51:58
M35-39	1:02:08	6:43	5:03:36	2:28	3:05:12	9:20:05
M35-39	54:21:00	6:11	4:58:49	2:47	3:24:28	9:26:35
M35-39	52:25:00	5:33	5:18:20	1:36	3:25:47	9:43:39
M35-39	1:02:03	6:04	5:25:28	2:49	3:13:06	9:49:28
M35-39	1:06:43	6:36	5:14:00	3:29	3:18:50	9:49:36
M35-39	1:05:03	6:30	5:18:57	2:13	3:17:41	9:50:22
M35-39	1:01:12	6:47	5:21:01	2:42	3:18:58	9:50:38
M35-39	56:59:00	6:27	5:22:04	2:54	3:24:56	9:53:19
M35-39	54:33:00	5:25	5:20:13	1:54	3:32:19	9:54:22
M40-44	54:29:00	5:49	5:11:46	2:55	3:25:57	9:40:52
M40-44	58:44:00	5:50	5:18:17	2:15	3:16:38	9:41:42
M40-44	1:13:35	6:34	5:07:40	2:20	3:15:37	9:45:43
M40-44	57:26:00	4:59	5:14:19	2:31	3:32:28	9:51:40
M40-44	59:37:00	7:22	5:31:01	2:13	3:15:50	9:56:01
M40-44	1:01:12	6:09	5:11:54	3:29	3:33:41	9:56:23
M40-44	1:07:40	10:30	5:10:24	2:58	3:25:36	9:57:07
M40-44	1:10:44	7:25	5:18:12	3:05	3:23:44	10:03:08
M45-49	56:03:00	5:54	5:14:36	2:52	3:14:13	9:33:36
M45-49	1:07:52	7:57	5:13:45	2:29	3:41:03	10:13:05
M45-49	1:13:07	6:33	5:24:50	2:15	3:37:08	10:23:51
M45-49	1:11:47	6:54	5:31:10	3:53	3:39:28	10:33:11
M45-49	54:39:00	6:16	5:43:26	4:22	3:45:20	10:34:01
M45-49	1:07:53	7:51	5:26:54	8:23	3:45:17	10:36:17

Ironman Wisconsin 2008 Qualifying Times						
Division	Swim	T1	Bike	T2	Run	Total
M50-54	52:42:00	6:36	5:36:53	3:45	3:32:35	10:12:29
M50-54	1:00:40	7:49	5:32:51	2:32	3:32:56	10:16:46
M50-54	1:03:59	6:08	5:27:51	3:50	3:39:20	10:21:06
M50-54	1:14:31	7:07	5:16:11	2:55	3:54:25	10:35:06
M55-59	56:05:00	6:09	5:27:56	3:09	3:41:42	10:14:59
M55-59	1:07:56	6:40	5:43:01	3:40	4:04:45	11:06:00
M60-64	1:11:10	6:51	5:41:30	3:29	4:40:42	11:43:41
M65-69	1:24:23	13:58	6:14:48	7:46	4:35:59	12:36:52
M70-74	1:39:41	9:06	7:00:18	6:48	5:19:22	14:15:13
MPRO	51:52:00	4:26	4:48:41	1:53	2:56:40	8:43:29
MPRO	1:00:17	4:48	4:51:34	2:10	2:57:03	8:55:50
MPRO	55:21:00	4:08	5:04:31	2:08	2:53:34	8:59:39
MPRO	51:55:00	4:22	4:56:21	2:15	3:07:05	9:01:56
W18-24	57:48:00	6:48	5:49:33	3:39	3:49:44	10:47:29
W25-29	1:09:54	6:33	5:46:59	3:01	3:36:57	10:43:22
W25-29	58:41:00	6:47	6:12:10	3:50	3:54:33	11:15:59
W25-29	1:06:52	6:51	5:56:51	3:15	4:04:16	11:18:03
W30-34	1:04:15	5:42	5:48:19	2:55	3:32:28	10:33:37
W30-34	1:12:18	7:42	5:38:02	3:22	3:37:02	10:38:24
W30-34	54:21:00	6:27	6:00:07	3:50	3:48:25	10:53:09
W35-39	1:04:36	7:04	5:57:12	4:57	3:51:09	11:04:56
W35-39	1:10:22	8:06	6:05:20	3:13	3:38:16	11:05:17
W35-39	1:02:19	6:20	6:17:03	7:53	3:42:14	11:15:47
W35-39	1:18:23	9:06	5:56:54	2:42	3:55:49	11:22:52
W40-44	1:10:18	5:24	5:34:21	3:37	3:41:15	10:34:52
W40-44	1:01:54	5:58	5:57:13	2:48	3:41:57	10:49:49
W40-44	1:07:41	5:50	5:52:17	4:46	3:47:55	10:58:28
W45-49	1:08:56	6:27	5:51:59	3:27	3:33:53	10:44:41
W45-49	1:14:16	10:05	5:55:17	3:51	4:13:26	11:36:53
W50-54	1:05:26	8:16	6:11:26	4:26	4:16:23	11:45:56
W55-59	1:15:18	11:45	7:04:39	4:49	5:13:13	13:49:42
W60-64	1:08:54	11:40	7:05:24	4:53	5:55:38	14:26:28
WPRO	52:11:00	4:52	5:21:50	2:10	3:26:24	9:47:25
WPRO	1:04:33	5:37	5:13:01	2:14	3:24:23	9:49:46
WPRO	1:07:37	4:35	5:17:53	3:01	3:17:41	9:50:45

Ironman Florida 2008 Qualifying Times					
Division	Swim	T1	Bike	T2	Run	Total
M18-24	54:13:00	3:11	4:49:25	7:20	3:03:28	8:57:37
M18-24	1:04:07	5:00	4:44:56	1:57	3:12:17	9:08:16
M25-29	56:25:00	2:42	4:50:10	2:45	3:10:12	9:02:12
M25-29	53:53:00	4:59	4:51:54	3:29	3:13:29	9:07:41
M25-29	54:50:00	3:12	5:03:13	3:28	3:15:06	9:19:48
M30-34	58:36:00	3:13	4:58:44	2:32	2:58:25	9:01:27
M30-34	57:23:00	4:12	4:58:55	2:54	3:02:12	9:05:33
M30-34	1:04:29	5:25	4:57:31	2:41	3:02:21	9:12:26
M30-34	56:22:00	6:33	4:46:38	3:27	3:20:44	9:13:42
M30-34	1:03:04	4:14	4:48:00	1:47	3:20:40	9:17:42
M30-34	57:20:00	2:46	4:49:42	2:17	3:27:49	9:19:53
M35-39	56:34:00	3:45	4:48:55	1:54	3:02:25	8:53:30
M35-39	57:33:00	3:12	4:50:04	2:13	3:14:34	9:07:34
M35-39	58:17:00	3:41	5:06:37	3:02	2:58:21	9:09:56
M35-39	55:33:00	3:10	4:45:43	1:57	3:25:43	9:12:05
M35-39	55:28:00	4:44	4:49:11	4:11	3:19:12	9:12:44
M35-39	1:08:03	3:38	4:56:23	3:50	3:10:01	9:21:54
M35-39	1:00:50	3:02	4:59:27	2:05	3:21:19	9:26:41
M35-39	53:00:00	2:54	4:55:38	3:17	3:32:35	9:27:24
M40-44	55:34:00	3:44	4:46:14	4:42	3:10:30	9:00:42
M40-44	59:40:00	3:09	4:46:06	1:21	3:22:44	9:12:57
M40-44	59:21:00	4:19	4:56:11	2:53	3:14:13	9:16:56
M40-44	1:05:37	4:43	4:54:28	2:10	3:10:36	9:17:33
M40-44	57:06:00	3:58	4:59:01	2:16	3:16:04	9:18:22
M40-44	58:27:00	5:28	4:56:35	3:06	3:19:47	9:23:21
M40-44	56:06:00	4:01	4:52:10	3:20	3:28:23	9:23:59
M40-44	1:06:16	4:33	5:00:09	3:21	3:15:25	9:29:42
M40-44	1:01:50	4:27	4:57:24	2:03	3:25:30	9:31:13
M45-49	56:18:00	3:34	4:49:33	2:19	3:22:57	9:14:38
M45-49	53:54:00	2:48	4:54:44	2:21	3:41:06	9:34:51
M45-49	1:02:58	4:48	5:03:51	3:26	3:19:59	9:34:59
M45-49	1:04:19	4:46	4:55:33	4:12	3:30:44	9:39:33
M45-49	1:05:46	6:02	4:55:53	2:35	3:39:38	9:49:53
M45-49	1:01:14	5:46	5:08:39	2:59	3:34:20	9:52:56
M45-49	1:02:21	4:58	5:10:56	2:33	3:32:34	9:53:19

Ironman Florida 2008 Qualifying Times						
Division	Swim	T1	Bike	T2	Run	Total
M50-54	1:02:08	5:16	4:42:01	2:54	3:20:24	9:12:4
M50-54	1:02:19	4:32	4:48:25	4:34	3:37:03	9:36:5
M50-54	1:01:13	5:22	5:00:57	3:43	3:26:44	9:37:5
M50-54	1:17:00	5:13	4:54:36	3:57	3:26:59	9:47:4
M50-54	1:12:44	4:51	5:12:09	2:42	3:25:54	9:58:1
M55-59	1:03:29	4:10	4:54:33	3:39	3:41:21	9:47:1
M55-59	58:01:00	3:18	5:06:40	3:17	3:41:32	9:52:4
M60-64	1:15:19	8:49	5:22:59	8:26	4:01:11	10:56:4
M65-69	1:27:29	6:52	6:11:21	4:34	5:07:07	12:57:2
M70-74	1:19:55	9:03	6:29:18	8:23	5:36:03	13:42:3
M75-79	1:26:47	15:46	6:54:49	14:29	6:52:38	15:44:2
MPRO	48:15:00	1:44	4:19:00	1:44	2:57:19	8:07:5
MPRO	48:30:00	2:05	4:21:31	2:14	3:03:33	8:17:5
MPRO	53:18:00	2:18	4:29:34	2:16	2:55:37	8:23:0
MPRO	53:15:00	2:10	4:25:13	1:41	3:02:25	8:24:4
MPRO	51:16:00	2:10	4:30:26	1:49	2:59:56	8:25:3
W18-24	1:00:09	2:53	5:29:08	2:45	3:55:44	10:30:3
W25-29	55:06:00	2:55	5:28:09	2:28	3:37:07	10:05:4
W25-29	1:00:39	2:17	5:04:46	1:51	3:57:08	10:06:4
W30-34	1:01:14	4:24	5:26:09	2:53	3:23:58	9:58:3
W30-34	1:05:36	4:26	5:13:59	3:00	3:32:48	9:59:4
W30-34	1:11:06	4:34	5:17:07	2:52	3:30:18	10:05:5
W35-39	1:04:21	5:00	5:07:13	2:43	3:36:45	9:56:0
W35-39	1:10:26	3:11	5:09:59	2:59	3:30:21	9:56:5
W35-39	1:04:31	3:54	5:13:02	3:45	4:00:36	10:25:4
W35-39	1:14:36	4:32	5:13:21	3:25	3:54:02	10:29:5
W40-44	1:01:48	4:01	5:12:11	3:21	3:41:39	10:02:5
W40-44	1:08:56	4:16	5:17:35	4:23	3:52:42	10:27:5
W40-44	1:06:54	4:32	5:21:16	4:03	3:55:11	10:31:5
W45-49	1:00:06	5:27	5:02:52	2:39	3:59:58	10:10:5
W45-49	1:02:15	4:49	5:25:38	4:20	3:56:06	10:33:0
W45-49	1:09:55	5:25	5:14:48	2:13	4:06:40	10:39:0
W50-54	1:06:49	4:51	5:18:59	3:46	3:48:31	10:22:5
W55-59	1:16:33	6:04	5:31:02	3:37	4:46:45	11:43:5
W60-64	1:21:51	6:40	6:13:28	4:03	5:03:48	12:49:4
WPRO	59:10:00	1:46	5:04:25	2:00	3:06:56	9:14:1
WPRO	53:16:00	2:31	5:05:50	2:10	3:23:00	9:26:4

Ironman Coeur d'Alene 2009 Qualifying Times						
Division	Swim	T1	Bike	T2	Run	Total
M18-24	1:03:11	4:33	5:02:56	1:59	3:34:36	9:47:14
M25-29	1:00:00	2:52	5:02:26	1:42	3:24:11	9:31:09
M25-29	56:25:00	4:12	5:15:39	3:30	3:15:50	9:35:34
M25-29	1:11:12	3:17	5:09:00	1:36	3:11:55	9:36:58
M25-29	55:35:00	3:02	5:19:54	1:39	3:23:05	9:43:12
M30-34	1:00:08	6:20	4:54:43	1:58	3:07:51	9:10:58
M30-34	59:55:00	2:25	5:12:55	2:04	2:55:36	9:12:52
M30-34	56:24:00	3:08	5:03:37	1:42	3:17:08	9:21:57
M30-34	58:23:00	3:52	5:08:23	1:13	3:12:05	9:23:54
M30-34	1:03:44	5:18	5:01:07	3:14	3:16:14	9:29:35
M30-34	1:03:35	3:39	5:27:02	2:14	2:57:56	9:34:24
M35-39	1:03:13	4:06	5:07:34	1:30	3:08:11	9:24:31
M35-39	59:58:00	4:02	5:11:09	1:28	3:22:56	9:39:32
M35-39	1:04:44	3:42	5:13:57	1:35	3:18:26	9:42:22
M35-39	1:04:45	3:47	5:07:30	2:10	3:28:31	9:46:41
M35-39	1:08:52	5:10	5:25:12	1:57	3:05:37	9:46:46
M35-39	1:04:22	3:24	5:21:38	2:02	3:16:55	9:48:19
M35-39	1:03:42	4:39	5:14:28	1:43	3:24:34	9:49:04
M35-39	1:06:27	2:39	5:17:40	1:40	3:24:17	9:52:41
M40-44	1:02:42	3:51	5:12:41	1:32	3:16:39	9:37:22
M40-44	1:02:52	4:11	5:22:46	2:02	3:11:55	9:43:44
M40-44	1:09:14	3:36	5:08:18	2:01	3:26:54	9:50:01
M40-44	1:00:52	4:14	5:10:30	2:11	3:34:27	9:52:12
M40-44	1:04:49	3:15	5:16:25	5:09	3:24:43	9:54:19
M40-44	1:03:03	4:26	5:08:24	3:29	3:36:09	9:55:28
M40-44	1:03:39	3:23	5:18:54	1:53	3:28:10	9:55:57
M40-44	1:12:10	4:56	5:13:00	2:14	3:26:17	9:58:36
M40-44	1:01:24	3:27	5:13:44	3:54	3:39:55	10:02:22
M45-49	55:17:00	2:45	5:17:21	2:11	3:18:54	9:36:26
M45-49	59:55:00	3:17	5:27:18	2:19	3:31:15	10:04:02
M45-49	1:03:22	3:14	5:16:00	2:32	3:41:08	10:06:15
M45-49	1:16:42	4:26	5:20:06	2:20	3:25:27	10:08:59
M45-49	1:13:06	3:58	5:31:50	1:47	3:23:17	10:13:56
M45-49	59:05:00	4:54	5:12:48	2:05	3:55:10	10:13:59
M45-49	1:07:09	4:13	5:32:47	1:26	3:28:45	10:14:19

Qualifying for Kona 209

Ironman Coeur d'Alene 2009 Qualifying Times						
Division	Swim	T1	Bike	T2	Run	Total
M50-54	1:09:33	5:24	5:20:09	3:01	3:18:47	9:56:52
M50-54	1:15:58	3:32	5:26:59	1:44	3:17:23	10:05:34
M50-54	1:11:37	6:59	5:34:57	2:03	3:34:29	10:30:03
M50-54	1:03:19	5:09	5:42:32	2:15	3:43:29	10:36:42
M55-59	1:09:39	8:07	5:25:12	2:10	3:37:34	10:22:40
M55-59	1:18:33	6:17	5:26:47	2:31	3:55:59	10:50:06
M60-64	1:23:10	5:51	5:56:00	4:12	4:50:16	12:19:27
M65-69	1:11:32	5:31	6:38:47	2:09	4:47:47	12:45:44
M70-74	1:29:33	10:29	6:41:50	7:32	5:05:35	13:34:58
MPRO	50:28:00	2:03	4:40:42	1:10	2:57:51	8:32:12
MPRO	56:07:00	2:21	4:41:50	1:14	3:00:33	8:42:03
MPRO	59:48:00	2:14	4:52:29	1:18	2:54:31	8:50:19
MPRO	1:12:52	2:07	4:50:11	1:28	2:49:33	8:56:08
W18-24	1:03:29	3:32	5:48:32	2:34	3:29:20	10:27:26
W25-29	1:16:06	4:44	5:50:46	2:18	3:34:52	10:48:44
W25-29	1:18:55	5:51	5:42:14	2:19	3:49:22	10:58:40
W25-29	1:21:43	4:45	6:05:58	2:53	3:34:18	11:09:35
W30-34	1:08:05	4:50	5:48:14	2:59	3:49:13	10:53:19
W30-34	54:47:00	4:39	6:09:50	2:30	3:45:23	10:57:07
W30-34	1:13:00	3:47	5:56:50	2:56	3:43:01	10:59:31
W35-39	1:15:08	4:50	5:53:59	3:19	3:25:23	10:42:36
W35-39	1:09:17	4:06	5:41:31	1:43	3:51:17	10:47:52
W35-39	1:07:37	6:12	5:37:42	3:17	4:06:39	11:01:25
W35-39	1:12:15	8:21	5:43:44	4:47	4:01:23	11:10:28
W40-44	1:01:04	3:19	5:36:50	2:10	3:52:48	10:36:08
W40-44	59:59:00	3:21	5:43:52	2:00	3:52:43	10:41:53
W40-44	1:07:29	4:38	5:35:16	3:19	4:06:47	10:57:27
W40-44	1:09:50	6:21	5:54:10	3:07	3:47:18	11:00:44
W45-49	1:18:42	5:06	5:56:36	3:11	4:03:05	11:26:38
W45-49	1:22:43	5:14	6:09:23	2:13	3:49:20	11:28:51
W45-49	1:03:08	6:05	6:05:10	4:16	4:13:32	11:32:09
W50-54	1:19:17	4:27	6:05:48	2:25	4:27:17	11:59:13
W55-59	1:21:24	6:04	6:34:28	3:16	4:11:31	12:16:40
W60-64	1:31:02	7:42	6:40:27	3:40	5:17:41	13:40:30
WPRO	1:04:38	2:35	4:59:36	1:06	3:15:29	9:23:21
WPRO	58:29:00	2:29	5:16:26	0:53	3:13:55	9:32:10
WPRO	58:35:00	2:26	5:12:42	1:35	3:19:08	9:34:24

Ironman Lake Placid 2009 Qualifying Times						
Division	Swim	T1	Bike	T2	Run	Total
M18-24	57:25:00	4:19	5:34:41	2:59	3:10:29	9:49:51
M25-29	1:04:41	4:40	5:12:23	1:34	3:17:49	9:41:04
M25-29	1:00:52	4:59	5:15:41	2:43	3:24:47	9:49:01
M25-29	58:40:00	4:38	5:31:50	3:19	3:22:10	10:00:35
M30-34	54:11:00	5:21	5:12:04	2:08	3:35:13	9:48:56
M30-34	59:08:00	4:29	5:33:44	1:58	3:14:25	9:53:43
M30-34	58:13:00	4:35	5:28:39	1:32	3:21:08	9:54:05
M30-34	1:03:08	5:05	5:29:16	1:54	3:18:12	9:57:34
M30-34	1:05:26	5:09	5:23:04	3:23	3:21:57	9:58:58
M35-39	1:04:25	4:04	5:13:09	1:41	3:09:40	9:32:56
M35-39	52:14:00	4:17	5:21:52	3:31	3:24:37	9:46:29
M35-39	1:11:06	5:18	5:21:31	2:09	3:08:03	9:48:04
M35-39	58:52:00	6:03	5:23:47	2:28	3:20:32	9:51:40
M35-39	57:27:00	4:30	5:26:49	2:57	3:22:14	9:53:56
M35-39	1:08:25	4:08	5:31:07	2:15	3:13:26	9:59:20
M35-39	1:02:18	4:40	5:28:32	2:11	3:30:28	10:08:06
M35-39	1:03:11	4:45	5:29:35	1:18	3:29:57	10:08:44
M40-44	55:32:00	4:52	5:02:43	1:58	3:13:54	9:18:58
M40-44	1:03:16	5:07	5:31:01	2:01	3:16:04	9:57:27
M40-44	57:41:00	4:51	5:29:48	2:48	3:22:50	9:57:55
M40-44	52:16:00	5:19	5:43:28	3:46	3:14:25	9:59:14
M40-44	56:16:00	5:14	5:29:25	2:56	3:27:32	10:01:21
M40-44	1:00:54	6:04	5:31:13	4:08	3:24:48	10:07:06
M40-44	56:06:00	4:25	5:26:35	2:37	3:39:34	10:09:14
M40-44	58:07:00	4:08	5:34:55	3:23	3:30:07	10:10:38
M40-44	59:36:00	5:45	5:21:30	3:04	3:42:18	10:12:11
M45-49	55:45:00	5:21	5:27:43	3:33	3:27:12	9:59:32
M45-49	1:08:14	5:26	5:41:20	3:08	3:12:59	10:11:05
M45-49	58:04:00	6:17	5:36:30	2:27	3:34:14	10:17:30
M45-49	1:03:17	4:18	5:27:24	3:04	3:40:53	10:18:55
M45-49	57:38:00	5:57	5:33:46	2:41	3:42:35	10:22:35
M45-49	1:06:02	6:43	5:30:37	2:31	3:45:36	10:31:26
M45-49	59:57:00	5:22	5:34:50	3:27	3:49:02	10:32:35
M45-49	1:06:37	8:57	5:47:04	3:26	3:30:56	10:36:57

Ironman Lake Placid 2009 Qualifying Times					
Division	Swim	T1	Bike	T2	Run	Total
M50-54	57:01:00	4:51	5:21:45	3:34	3:30:39	9:57:47
M50-54	1:10:15	6:46	5:35:30	2:49	3:31:39	10:26:57
M50-54	59:49:00	4:34	5:51:41	3:18	3:34:57	10:34:17
M50-54	1:11:47	9:05	5:44:38	5:46	3:51:08	11:02:21
M50-54	1:08:27	8:32	5:39:51	3:59	4:08:45	11:09:33
M55-59	1:03:41	9:02	5:42:24	4:18	4:03:23	11:02:47
M55-59	1:14:52	8:14	5:49:39	3:42	3:52:38	11:09:04
M55-59	1:07:49	7:58	5:39:09	2:28	4:22:15	11:19:37
M60-64	1:18:00	9:23	7:13:55	8:32	5:06:06	13:55:54
M65-69	1:42:15	8:24	7:44:00	19:16	6:08:47	16:02:40
M70-74	1:23:32	9:13	7:05:21	3:43	5:36:57	14:18:45
MPRO	55:47:00	3:29	4:53:56	1:08	3:02:17	8:56:35
MPRO	51:50:00	3:30	4:54:08	2:38	3:10:26	9:02:31
MPRO	1:05:43	2:54	5:03:22	1:43	2:58:30	9:12:09
MPRO	55:42:00	3:32	5:20:34	1:32	2:54:09	9:15:27
W18-24	1:18:56	13:13	6:48:39	6:52	4:05:58	12:33:37
W25-29	1:01:49	4:55	5:55:26	2:29	3:51:20	10:55:57
W25-29	1:19:25	5:14	5:56:24	3:35	4:09:48	11:34:23
W30-34	1:07:07	5:53	5:29:45	1:56	3:51:22	10:36:01
W30-34	1:09:32	4:54	5:47:49	1:59	3:34:59	10:39:10
W30-34	1:08:53	5:32	5:40:51	2:49	3:50:46	10:48:49
W30-34	1:09:38	5:38	5:58:01	3:08	3:49:41	11:06:04
W35-39	1:01:58	5:13	5:49:49	2:22	3:42:31	10:41:52
W35-39	57:47:00	5:21	5:50:23	3:54	3:49:01	10:46:24
W35-39	1:09:17	6:06	6:02:17	2:43	3:50:45	11:11:06
W40-44	53:38:00	4:14	5:51:24	1:54	3:23:13	10:14:22
W40-44	1:05:13	4:52	6:01:12	2:27	3:53:35	11:07:17
W40-44	1:03:07	4:26	5:45:46	2:58	4:11:43	11:07:58
W40-44	1:06:43	5:53	6:15:29	2:44	3:46:03	11:16:50
W45-49	1:18:28	6:43	6:02:27	4:05	3:42:23	11:14:04
W45-49	1:03:13	6:49	6:16:14	3:15	4:00:08	11:29:38
W45-49	1:24:04	6:32	6:06:45	4:06	4:00:01	11:41:26
W50-54	1:06:19	5:54	5:56:35	2:46	4:15:21	11:26:54
W50-54	1:05:12	6:24	6:28:42	3:56	4:04:55	11:49:06
W55-59	1:25:24	9:01	7:02:04	5:49	5:15:45	13:58:02
WPRO	55:11:00	4:34	5:43:10	1:23	2:57:05	9:41:21
WPRO	55:41:00	3:11	5:28:45	1:15	3:15:36	9:44:24
WPRO	1:05:35	4:20	5:26:51	2:18	3:26:58	10:05:59

Ironman Canada 2009 Qualifying Times						
Division	Swim	T1	Bike	T2	Run	Total
M18-24	59:50:00	2:52	5:24:17	2:39	3:36:54	10:06:30
M25-29	52:57:00	2:59	4:58:06	2:46	3:53:51	9:50:36
M25-29	1:02:16	2:56	5:11:01	2:31	3:33:37	9:52:19
M25-29	1:00:49	2:38	5:14:04	3:50	3:31:57	9:53:17
M30-34	59:37:00	3:46	5:10:42	1:44	3:19:10	9:34:58
M30-34	1:07:10	3:07	5:12:41	2:00	3:18:50	9:43:47
M30-34	1:00:24	2:35	5:11:30	1:29	3:34:54	9:50:50
M30-34	1:04:15	3:06	5:26:14	2:13	3:22:10	9:57:56
M30-34	1:03:30	3:13	5:19:47	2:09	3:41:15	10:09:52
M35-39	55:33:00	2:27	5:14:53	3:32	3:26:29	9:42:52
M35-39	1:01:17	2:46	5:19:24	4:21	3:20:57	9:48:43
M35-39	1:03:21	2:57	5:13:46	2:44	3:26:37	9:49:22
M35-39	1:06:44	3:06	5:17:15	3:13	3:31:30	10:01:46
M35-39	1:00:52	3:13	5:22:33	2:44	3:36:19	10:05:40
M35-39	54:47:00	2:29	5:22:11	2:45	3:49:23	10:11:34
M35-39	1:13:05	6:25	5:10:30	2:38	3:39:35	10:12:11
M35-39	1:09:51	4:07	5:16:58	2:45	3:41:02	10:14:42
M40-44	1:06:47	3:02	5:15:30	3:07	3:22:41	9:51:06
M40-44	1:14:06	3:09	5:09:09	3:57	3:25:25	9:55:44
M40-44	1:00:00	3:29	5:16:13	3:04	3:34:34	9:57:18
M40-44	1:06:34	3:06	5:27:26	3:33	3:20:40	10:01:17
M40-44	1:13:31	3:58	5:13:08	3:22	3:30:03	10:04:00
M40-44	1:08:49	3:44	5:13:22	3:23	3:35:48	10:05:05
M40-44	1:11:21	2:59	5:08:16	3:46	3:42:04	10:08:24
M40-44	1:04:50	3:28	5:36:43	3:28	3:27:09	10:15:37
M45-49	1:05:27	2:49	5:23:06	2:24	3:29:21	10:03:04
M45-49	1:05:30	2:46	5:23:40	2:03	3:34:01	10:07:58
M45-49	55:33:00	3:49	5:18:57	2:35	3:48:15	10:09:07
M45-49	59:17:00	2:39	5:28:05	5:32	3:46:08	10:21:40
M45-49	1:09:48	4:12	5:31:43	2:28	3:37:41	10:25:50
M45-49	1:04:24	3:18	5:34:32	2:13	3:44:02	10:28:27
M45-49	1:09:41	3:25	5:32:55	2:31	3:42:05	10:30:34

Ironman Canada 2009 Qualifying Times						
Division	Swim	T1	Bike	T2	Run	Total
M50-54	58:57:00	3:46	5:22:35	5:09	3:50:57	10:21:22
M50-54	1:17:21	3:09	5:21:42	4:01	3:43:01	10:29:12
M50-54	1:05:14	2:56	5:24:03	4:50	3:58:07	10:35:08
M50-54	1:09:22	3:39	5:40:32	4:09	3:41:06	10:38:47
M50-54	1:10:48	4:18	5:43:44	3:04	3:46:34	10:48:26
M55-59	1:09:29	3:58	5:40:08	4:08	3:55:28	10:53:10
M55-59	1:09:51	3:24	5:48:11	3:17	4:15:53	11:20:33
M55-59	1:18:54	3:39	5:51:57	4:19	4:07:11	11:25:59
M60-64	1:22:14	4:45	5:48:49	3:20	4:56:11	12:15:17
M60-64	1:22:31	4:52	6:23:10	6:50	4:32:01	12:29:23
M65-69	1:23:10	4:51	6:29:36	6:14	4:43:39	12:47:28
MPRO	48:40:00	1:46	4:47:22	1:30	3:01:00	8:40:17
MPRO	53:09:00	1:25	4:55:24	1:44	2:56:49	8:48:29
MPRO	48:38:00	1:36	4:45:46	2:48	3:20:48	8:59:34
MPRO	54:24:00	1:46	4:50:35	2:25	3:13:37	9:02:45
MPRO	46:23:00	1:40	4:46:53	1:58	3:27:06	9:03:59
W18-24	1:04:05	2:27	5:35:44	1:38	4:23:34	11:07:26
W25-29	1:12:04	2:47	5:35:47	2:10	3:54:02	10:46:49
W25-29	1:08:33	3:32	5:45:58	3:33	3:59:16	11:00:51
W30-34	1:16:06	2:30	5:40:15	2:01	3:28:15	10:29:04
W30-34	55:41:00	2:10	5:42:07	2:47	3:55:58	10:38:41
W30-34	1:02:40	2:51	5:42:11	2:24	3:50:27	10:40:31
W35-39	1:04:21	2:33	5:25:02	1:55	3:42:43	10:16:33
W35-39	55:43:00	2:32	5:40:21	3:08	3:35:49	10:17:31
W35-39	1:10:16	3:03	5:47:03	3:10	3:34:32	10:38:02
W35-39	1:07:11	2:15	5:54:04	2:21	3:46:09	10:51:57
W40-44	1:09:59	4:07	5:23:10	3:02	3:46:29	10:26:44
W40-44	1:08:44	4:25	5:26:21	2:41	3:45:47	10:27:57
W40-44	1:03:47	2:19	5:28:08	2:24	3:52:44	10:29:20
W40-44	1:01:17	2:57	5:27:55	3:53	4:03:21	10:39:21
W45-49	1:27:03	3:46	5:50:16	3:46	3:50:06	11:14:56
W45-49	1:19:42	5:32	5:58:40	4:16	3:58:58	11:27:06
W45-49	1:06:27	3:00	6:18:59	6:51	3:57:15	11:32:31
W50-54	1:23:18	2:56	5:57:46	3:16	4:12:49	11:40:02
W50-54	1:01:44	3:30	5:48:16	4:10	4:49:52	11:47:31
W55-59	1:14:47	7:43	6:23:51	8:50	4:33:27	12:28:36
W60-64	1:26:45	6:41	7:20:16	8:57	5:22:33	14:25:12
W75+	1:33:04	7:41	7:44:49	14:15	7:14:43	16:54:30
WPRO	53:18:00	1:48	5:12:20	1:43	3:31:42	9:40:48
WPRO	1:01:12	1:57	5:22:07	1:22	3:26:59	9:53:35

Ironman Louisville 2009 Qualifying Times					
Division	Swim	T1	Bike	T2	Run	Total
M18-24	1:11:30	3:06	5:09:36	2:57	3:21:20	9:48:29
M18-24	1:12:40	3:42	5:12:53	4:23	3:45:22	10:19:00
M18-24	1:13:48	3:46	5:22:56	3:51	3:42:37	10:26:59
M25-29	51:11:00	4:23	5:00:07	4:26	3:08:40	9:08:47
M25-29	58:07:00	3:49	5:15:48	2:59	3:18:06	9:38:49
M25-29	1:08:26	4:33	5:07:36	4:09	3:17:32	9:42:17
M25-29	1:01:05	2:56	5:14:46	5:55	3:20:51	9:45:34
M25-29	1:15:52	3:50	5:12:17	3:32	3:16:50	9:52:22
M30-34	1:09:00	3:28	5:03:44	2:35	3:14:51	9:33:39
M30-34	1:17:50	4:21	4:52:23	3:31	3:19:54	9:38:00
M30-34	55:49:00	4:54	5:18:27	3:25	3:19:00	9:41:35
M30-34	1:01:40	4:54	5:16:55	3:49	3:19:36	9:46:55
M30-34	1:14:25	4:36	5:12:48	3:50	3:12:14	9:47:53
M35-39	55:17:00	3:31	5:04:17	2:29	3:17:51	9:23:25
M35-39	58:33:00	2:44	5:18:49	2:50	3:03:23	9:26:19
M35-39	1:01:01	3:40	4:58:49	3:14	3:30:44	9:37:29
M35-39	1:02:18	3:53	5:09:22	4:08	3:28:25	9:48:06
M35-39	57:34:00	3:25	5:21:50	3:01	3:29:30	9:55:20
M35-39	1:12:07	3:34	5:12:34	2:43	3:24:28	9:55:27
M35-39	1:10:18	3:23	5:02:08	3:48	3:42:03	10:01:40
M35-39	1:09:14	4:23	5:11:08	3:40	3:33:18	10:01:44
M40-44	1:06:41	3:47	5:03:33	2:29	3:17:50	9:34:21
M40-44	1:03:53	4:35	5:12:34	5:59	3:17:10	9:44:11
M40-44	1:10:35	4:11	5:08:28	2:54	3:27:04	9:53:12
M40-44	1:05:33	4:20	5:18:04	5:17	3:22:49	9:56:04
M40-44	58:12:00	3:07	5:12:49	2:51	3:41:53	9:58:53
M40-44	1:03:48	4:51	5:19:44	5:14	3:28:15	10:01:53
M40-44	1:09:43	4:03	5:24:13	3:15	3:23:04	10:04:18
M40-44	1:13:16	3:49	5:14:14	4:42	3:35:18	10:11:20
M45-49	1:11:34	3:17	5:11:29	6:38	3:13:37	9:46:35
M45-49	1:19:05	4:30	5:09:53	2:56	3:21:53	9:58:18
M45-49	1:13:30	3:51	5:13:49	5:37	3:26:01	10:02:48
M45-49	56:52:00	3:22	5:30:01	4:08	3:32:54	10:07:17
M45-49	1:16:04	4:29	4:55:20	2:49	3:54:43	10:13:26

Ironman Louisville 2009 Qualifying Times					
Division	Swim	T1	Bike	T2	Run	Total

Division	Swim	T1	Bike	T2	Run	Total
M50-54	1:07:53	3:17	5:16:37	3:45	3:44:28	10:16:01
M50-54	1:21:16	7:31	5:15:58	5:11	3:31:29	10:21:26
M50-54	1:15:24	3:49	5:17:37	3:38	3:44:38	10:25:07
M55-59	1:06:20	4:04	5:28:00	2:58	4:11:09	10:52:31
M55-59	1:26:17	9:28	6:15:47	7:32	3:36:49	11:35:53
M60-64	1:11:43	5:46	5:53:52	6:30	4:05:30	11:23:21
M60-64	1:20:36	6:13	5:29:07	6:16	4:24:46	11:26:58
M65-69	1:42:17	8:40	5:49:07	7:03	5:05:54	12:53:02
M70-74	1:58:51	9:48	7:29:04	8:28	5:35:18	15:21:30
MPRO	53:05:00	2:09	4:43:47	2:14	3:02:21	8:43:36
MPRO	44:54:00	2:32	4:54:19	2:27	3:08:55	8:53:07
MPRO	48:30:00	2:28	5:04:01	3:20	2:56:41	8:55:00
MPRO	48:36:00	2:31	4:47:50	3:35	3:19:03	9:01:35
MPRO	57:49:00	3:13	4:59:47	2:13	3:06:14	9:09:16
W25-29	1:07:49	4:22	5:26:05	3:10	3:33:37	10:15:04
W25-29	1:24:52	8:26	5:16:46	5:36	3:27:34	10:23:14
W25-29	1:03:10	4:45	5:40:20	3:36	3:42:01	10:33:53
W30-34	55:32:00	3:12	5:34:31	3:43	3:50:57	10:27:56
W30-34	1:00:24	3:24	5:44:58	4:35	3:37:13	10:30:35
W30-34	1:09:30	4:23	5:50:23	5:04	3:38:05	10:47:25
W35-39	57:26:00	4:04	5:31:45	4:35	3:33:45	10:11:36
W35-39	1:13:16	4:24	5:29:10	3:31	3:31:41	10:22:03
W35-39	1:09:03	3:23	5:41:24	4:12	3:25:21	10:23:24
W35-39	1:00:14	3:34	5:28:16	2:56	3:53:31	10:28:31
W40-44	1:09:06	3:58	5:35:45	3:37	3:54:19	10:46:46
W40-44	1:15:09	6:35	5:43:34	4:40	3:44:24	10:54:23
W40-44	1:23:12	3:51	5:34:26	5:12	4:04:50	11:11:32
W45-49	1:28:33	6:44	5:47:02	3:59	3:31:58	10:58:16
W45-49	1:29:22	5:55	5:48:38	4:44	4:00:06	11:28:45
W50-54	1:21:31	4:08	6:11:11	3:14	4:01:48	11:41:52
W50-54	1:43:31	8:27	6:17:20	7:18	3:50:02	12:06:39
W55-59	1:53:01	4:51	6:54:37	7:23	4:48:59	13:48:52
W60-64	1:32:22	11:25	6:45:59	13:46	6:09:36	14:53:08
WPRO	1:10:24	3:09	5:16:36	3:07	3:05:07	9:38:23
WPRO	59:56:00	3:21	5:31:53	3:58	3:21:14	10:00:22
WPRO	1:00:41	2:52	5:53:17	2:53	3:26:18	10:26:01

About the Author

Raymond Britt is Managing Partner at WinSight Ventures, publisher of RunTri.com and one of the most experienced endurance athletes in the world.

Few can match Britt's extensive competitive record. He's completed 29 Ironman Triathlons (2.4 mile swim, 112 mile bike ride, 26.2 mile run), 48 Marathons, 8 Ultramarathons (31 or more miles) and more than 60 other triathlons and running races.

Since his debut race – the 1994 Chicago Marathon – Britt has covered nearly 50,000 training and racing miles around the globe. He's finished the Chicago Marathon 12 times, the Boston Marathon 13 consecutive times, Hawaii Ironman World Championships 3 times, and has been a USA Triathlon All-American.

Britt's, articles, photographs and perspectives have been featured by CNN, NBC, New York Times, USA Today, Chicago Tribune, Chicago Sun-Times, Los Angeles Times, Triathlete magazine, Running Times magazine and many others.

As publisher of RunTri.com, Britt serves an annual audience of 500,000 worldwide readers, providing free training and racing resources to help athletes achieve their goals.

6285551R0

Made in the USA
Lexington, KY
05 August 2010